Ruth + He
1 8 6 4 , 8 3

I hope you all
will like this
Book,
God Bless you Both

Grand maw Cash

Ruth Cash

MY EXPERIENCES IN SERVING GOD

BY REV. RUTH CASH

The following pages are just a few things I've experienced during my walk with God.

All the things I wrote are true, and I wouldn't write anything down that wasn't true.

To God be all the Glory and Honor.

— *Rev. Ruth Cash*

And Jesus went about all Galilee, teaching in their synagogues, and preaching the gospel of the kingdom, and healing all manner of sickness and all manner of disease among the people.
MATTHEW 4:23

Forward

BY J. R. COGDILL

E verybody's got a story. Ever since I was a child, I have been captivated by such amazing stories. I loved to read about superheroes and detectives, heroes who accomplished amazing things. It should come as no surprise then, that I became infatuated with the stories I learned in my Sunday School. God created the world in six days. Only the inhabitants of the ark survived the massive flood that God used to judge the world. The waters parted as Moses led God's people across the bed of the Red Sea. The sun refused to set as God gave victory to Joshua and his army. The mouths of the lions were sealed shut as Daniel spent a night in their den because of the prayers he lifted up to God.

A great transformation took place in my life as I learned these were not mere tales of fiction. These were true events that displayed the incredible power of a mighty God. Many people do not trust in the validity of these events. Such emphasis and attention are placed on fictional superheroes and other tales of fantasy, but many of these same people scoff at the thought of a miracle-working God. Even those who believe put the events of the Bible in some distant category without giving credence to God's power being active today.

Everybody's got a story. Some stories do not have much detail. One such story belongs to Enoch. He has only a handful of verses to tell his story in Genesis 5:19-24. These verses tell that he was the son of Jared. They tell us he was the father of Methuselah. They tell us he lived for 365 years. Most of these stories end with death. This story, however, ends differently. Scripture says that Enoch walked with God. Enoch did not die; rather "God took him." This brief recap provides a lot of speculation as to what happened to Enoch and why his story ended differently than so many other men who are mentioned in that same chapter.

However, Enoch's story is expanded upon in Hebrews 11:5-6. Hebrews explains that Enoch did not experience death because "...he had this testimony, that he pleased God."

Of all the incredible things that have happened in all the stories that have been told, fact or fiction, throughout the history of this world, this one statement brings focus to the purpose of life. What is our testimony? What story is our life telling?

What really influenced my life was the fact that, as I learned these Sunday School stories as a child, I got to see modern day stories being lived around me. One of these stories belonged to one of my early Sunday School teachers, Ruth Cash. Her testimonies and her dynamic relationship with God stood out for my young mind. When I made the decision to kneel at the altar and to ask Jesus to come into my life, Ruth Cash was kneeling by my side, leading me in that prayer. She has used her life to glorify God and many souls have been touched in the process.

The memories and testimonies she has compiled in this book is an incredible treasure. The modern day church benefits greatly from taking a peek at its heritage. The American landscape had changed dramatically in the last century in almost every aspect. The spiritual aspect of the country is no different. Jesus was a scholar of the scripture and of history. He had an incredible task ahead of Him, but He did not ignore what had occurred before Him. When studying our spiritual heritage, we would be foolish not to look at the generations before us and see the pioneering work that has been done by our parents, grandparents, great-grandparents and so on. As I read these testimonies and memoirs, my heart is blessed at how God blessed her childhood and then used her in ministry.

Everybody's got a story. This story belongs to Ruth Cash. But that's the thing about stories. So many of our stories interconnect. In truth, we're all part of one story. God's story.

And our goal should echo that which was achieved by Enoch.

By faith Enoch was translated that he should not see death; and was not found, because God had translated him: for before his translation he had this testimony, that he pleased God. But without faith, it is impossible to please him: for he that cometh to God must believe that he is, and that he is a rewarder of them that diligently seek him.

HEBREWS 11:5-6

Part One

My Experiences

BITS AND PIECES
EARLY EXPERIENCES

When I was three years old, my Daddy bought an A-model Ford car. He decided to go to Texas. He got a man named Mr. Hall to drive us because Daddy could not drive. Fred was the oldest son. James was the second boy. Ineze was the first girl. Christine was the second girl. And Ruth was the third girl; that was me.

Well, we got started to Texas. Mr. Hall drove. It came night and my Mama and my Daddy got out of the car and put quilts on the ground for us to sleep. When we all went to sleep, Mr. Hall drove off with the car and left us. The next morning, my Daddy took us down to the train station. He put us in a box car. The train pulled out.

I was three-years old at that time. I was still nursing. Well, I started crying because the milk wouldn't satisfy me. When the train stopped to get water, the conductor came back where we were. He said that he would have to put us off if I didn't stop crying. When the train stopped again, I was still crying, so he put us off. There was another man standing there. My Daddy said, "My friend, when they put you off the train, what do you do?" He said, "When the train starts, get back on."

Well, my Daddy started pitching us kids up to my brother, who would catch us. They all were in but me. When my Daddy pitched me up to my brother, he caught me by my dress tail as I started down under the wheel. We all got on the train and there were two boys running from the law. They got in the same box car we were in. We were all afraid. My Daddy said, "Be still." The boys weren't there long until they heard the law coming down beside the train. The two boys got on top of the train. The law caught them.

We finally got to Texas. My Daddy put a tent up. They had a wood cook stove. We had just enough food to make do with. They got a job picking cotton. While Mama and Daddy and Fred picked cotton, we stayed around about the camp. We went down to a house where some Mexicans lived and they were cooking chitlins. I can remember just as if it were yesterday. We went out in the pasture and there was a big jack rabbit. It went running out through the pasture. There was also a big bull. We ran as fast as we could. We slid under the fence and got to safety.

The people told my Daddy that sand storms would come up and, when they did, you better get in the storm pit. My Daddy saw a sand storm coming. He told my Mama to get in the storm pit. She said she wasn't going, so Daddy took us kids down. When we came out, the tent was blown down. My Mama's dress was over her head and her face was black as soot. My Daddy said, "I'll guess you'll go next time to the storm pit."

Well, there came a carnival to town. My Daddy took us to see it. The man asked my oldest brother to ride the old hog. He got on, but fell off. My younger brother jumped on and rode it. The man said he didn't ask him to ride, so he wouldn't give him any money.

Well the cotton was all picked and we got ready to come home. We went down to the train station. When the train pulled off, my Daddy began to pitch us kids to my brother. When we had gone a good distance, I started crying for water. The conductor stopped to get water and came back where we were. He said we would have to get off if I was crying when he stopped again. Well, we went a long way before the train stopped again. I was still crying. We were in town, so my Daddy and all of us got off. They sent us kids down to the bakery to get something to eat. They gave us some cakes. My Mama went down to the Salvation Army and they bought her and us three girls a ticket and put us on a bus to go home. Daddy and Fred and James had to hobo the rest of the way home.

After we got home, my Daddy went down to Mr. Johnson's to share crop. That is when a man buys seed and fertilizer and the man would get the third of the crop. One day, my Daddy and Mama got in a quarrel. Well, my Daddy started pitching dishes out the back door. My Mama went outside and got the ax. She came back in the house and started to bust the cook stove. My Daddy said, "Stop, Mama. Don't bust the stove. That's all we have to cook on." Well, my Daddy got us children and he told Mama he was going to take us down to the river and drown us. Well, he took us down to the river. I remember walking down the river road, but he didn't do anything. He just wanted to scare my mother.

When everything settled down, they planted the crops. Mr. Johnson had an eighteen-year old boy. He was bad to drink. Daddy was on the back porch with a straight razor and the boy was coming down the hill toward my Daddy with a machete. Daddy couldn't keep him off so he swung around and cut the tip of his lung. They took the boy to Dr. Gaston at Travelers Rest. He sewed up the cut place, but he didn't clean the wound. The boy died. Daddy had a lawyer, and the time come for him to go to court. The lawyer told my Daddy to plead guilty in self-defense, but he pleaded not guilty. He ended up with life in prison because he didn't listen to the lawyer. If he had listened, he would have went free.

Mama was about to have a child the day Daddy was to go to prison. Mama had to go to the shelter. Uncle Jess Batson and Mama started down the road. I was four-years old and I pulled all my clothes off and I was running down the road as fast as I could run. My aunt told Lee to catch me, so he did and Aunt Ida tore my hide up.

Well, when Mama got well enough to take care of the family, she rented an old log house down the hollow. You could see the chickens through the cracks of the floor. When it snowed, it would snow in on the bed. My mother and my brother James planted a garden and she plowed the garden with James right by her side. Mama and James would cut wood with a cross cut saw. They made fifty cents a day. Back then, we paid five cents for a coke. For one cent we got a bag of candy and for fifty cents a side of hog. My Mama would go through the woods to my Aunt Ida's house. She would churn for her, sweep the yard, and she would give Mama a gallon of milk and half a pound of butter. She would have to walk home. At the time, my baby sister was four-years old. We was out in the yard playing. We were swinging her by her arms and feet and we dropped her and broke her arm.

On Sunday, we would go with Uncle Jess to Church of the Brethren at Travelers Rest, SC. Uncle Jess was a Baptist preacher and sure did enjoy going to church. I remember when they would have the Lord's Supper. The women would wear a white cap that looked like mash cloth. Aunt Girt Peterson and Uncle Tom would cook a half of a beef and make sop. To make sop, you put loaf bread in the beef broth. They would eat, then they had unleavened bread and grape juice. Then they would wash feet - the men in one room and the women in one room.

My uncle would come a little ways out of Travelers Rest. We lived on White Horse Road. Uncle Carl would drive a wagon and come after us. We would go and stay with him a week. We sure did have a good time. Then it come time for us to go home. Mama and James would pick cotton for Mr. Springfield and I remember that was the first cotton I ever picked. I picked thirty pounds. I was six-years old. I sure was glad I could pick cotton.

One night we were down beside the bed praying and Mama looked up and there was a man looking in the window at us. James got the shot gun and he got in front of us. We left the house and went up to Mr. Springfield's house. We sure was afraid. Come to find out, the man was running from the law for trying to choke a woman to death. He folded rags and stuffed them down her throat. But they caught him.

One day my mother was over at Aunt Lola's working and it came up a storm. It sure did blow down big trees. Them trees were big. My sister Inez got the ax and went outside and cut a little pine tree. It was about the size of a woman's arm around her wrist. Boy, the wind was blowing. The chickens came in the house. The pig run under the bed and tore my mother's coat up. My mother was worried to death. But, thank God, He took care of us.

Well, Mama finally got the house cleaned up. Well, I caught the little chickens and pinched their heads off. Mama told me if I didn't stop, she was going to cut my fingers off. I kept killing them. She took me to the window and put my fingers under the window. She said, "If you don't stop killing the chickens, I'm going to cut your fingers off." I never killed no more chickens.

We went over to Aunt Lola's one day. When we started home, I cried all the way. Mama put me to bed. I went in a coma. She sent for Dr. Coleman. Stanley Coleman and T. E. Coleman were brothers. They came to our home for six weeks. They would bring their rabbit dogs and hunt when they come. They had a brand new A-model Rumble seat car. They began to give me medicine and they thought I had Typhoid Fever. But one day, after six weeks, I come out of it. The Lord took care of me.

When the garden was gathered, my mother rented a house on White Horse Road in Travelers Rest. The house belonged to Jim Evans. He planted cane. That is what somebody uses to make home-made syrup. They call it sorghum syrup. How they made it was to squeeze the cane and the juice that came out went down in a barrel. There was a pan they would use to boil the juice. When it was cooked down, they would pour it in jars. Now, the syrup that was made, that sure was good.

Now, winter come and Mama had corn on the cobb and also the cotton they had picked. She sold it and bought us one pair of shoes a year. We went to Ebenezer school. They had hot lunch. We had pinto beans, sliced onion, and corn bread. It sure was good. One time I had to stay in at recess. I was six-years old and I ate one of the children's lunch. When the teacher came back in, it was time to eat. The little girl went to get her lunch and I had eaten it. The teacher got my hand and she had a ruler. She sure did spank me. I never got nobody's lunch again.

We had to walk to school. When our shoes wore out, Mama would cut cardboard and put it in our shoes. We wore cotton stockings and home-made dresses. My mother even made our panties. We wore feed sack dresses. Now the feed sacks had flower designs on them.

In the winter, the icicles were everywhere down the side of the road. When we got to school, it felt like our hand would freeze off. They had an old pot belly stove and they used coal to heat with. Our hands were so cold that when we got next to the stove, they would hurt so bad. The schools weren't nice like our schools today. When we got home, Mama would have baked sweet potatoes, turnip greens, and milk cornbread. At night, we got our wood in and Mama milked the cow.

Then it came time to go to Wednesday night service. Mr. Lee Silvers would come by and pick us up. He had a logging truck. We got up on the truck right behind the cab. It had no side rails on it. We went up on Holiness Hill at Marietta, SC. We would have service and it would last till twelve or one o'clock at night. The women prayed one hour before service out in the woods. The men did the same. We really had wonderful meetings. We went up there till they made the Church of God down at Slater, S.C. My youngest brother was the first one got married in the new church.

My baby sister took sick and had to stay in bed. She wouldn't stay in bed unless I would stay in the bed with her. I remember my mother had a broom made of broom straw and she would sweep the floor. When she would get to where the fire place was and swap the hearth off, it would smell so good. My sister finally got well. Now my mother got my brother James a bicycle and he had a girlfriend up the road a piece. Those girls were not the kind of girls they ought to be. Well, James come home one day and Mama asked him where he had been so long. He got mad and drew back his hand to hit my mother. There was a brush broom lying there and she picked it up and hit James; it knocked him down and broke his watch. Mr. Jim Evans came up there where we were and he asked James if he would hit his mother.

There was a revival at Forestville Baptist Church and my mother didn't have a way to go that night. My mother's hair was partly gray, so she took black shoe polish and put it on her hair and they left to go to church. She rode the bike with my brother. One evening they started to the revival and it started to rain. The shoe polish run down her face.

After revival, they had an all-day singing and dinner on the ground. I remember how they would make lemonade in a number two-tin tub. We would eat, then they would sing. They would have saltine crackers and peanut butter. I thought that was the best thing I ever ate. Uncle Dave Frazier and Aunt Martha would come over to our house and Mama and Aunt Martha would go to the corn field to gather roasting ears, that is corn and tomatoes. They would cook dinner. Mama would kill a chicken to fry. They would even clean the feet and fry them. Boy, we would really eat. Everything was so good.

Then night would come and we would go to church. They didn't even worry about the time. We had lamp light and a wood cook stove. We would go out in the woods and drag up pine logs for the wood stove. Sometimes, we went out in the woods and hunt pine knots to start the fire because we couldn't get oil like people do today because we didn't have the money. Sometimes we would go to mother's brother's house to eat dinner. I would play so hard. When I come home, I would be sick. We heard about a Brush Harbor meeting. Now the brush harbor was made out of brush. They put pine brush limbs on top of slabs for us to sit on. They brought them from the saw mill. I remember I was seven and a half years old when I got saved in that old Brush Harbor.

When someone had a revival, we would go. It didn't matter what church it was – Baptist Church or Church of God. We would go. Mr. Lee Silvers would come after us. People would come from miles to the meeting. It didn't matter what time the service let out. Sometimes it would last till twelve or one in the morning. The women wore bonnets and aprons. Men wore overalls and a long sleeve blue shirt. Just about all men wore long sleeves and there wasn't as many colors as there are today. And if the preacher had a suit, the knees were worn out from praying. Now days, the seat is worn from sitting. I remember that people would give the preacher chickens or ham or vegetables out of the garden or canned goods for preaching. Just about everyone worked on the farm and money was hard to come by. My mother didn't work outside the home so there was no money coming in. The DSS gave food out to the ones that needed it. There wasn't any food stamps in those days. They give you flour, lard, corn meal, sugar, beans, rice, and fat back. We had plenty such as it was. My mother raised corn, tomatoes, cabbage, salad turnips, beets, onions, and chickens, so we were all happy.

My mother was invited to Aunt Martha Frazier's. They wanted to go fishing. When we got down there, us kids stayed at the house. Well, Uncle Frazier made moonshine liquor. He soaked some apples in the liquor and us kids found them. We ate some of them. We were sitting on the pig pen fence. Well, we got drunk and fell in the pig pen. When Mama and Mrs. Frazier came back, they found us kids in the pig pen. We were small. I was eight-years old. You know, kids will do anything.

It was time to go home now. Mama had to get wood in, milk the cow, and feed the chickens. We had to carry water from our neighbor's. Well, I remember they had a great big white grape vine and we would go down there and eat till we couldn't eat anymore. Daddy was still in prison in Columbia, SC. My mother was getting a paper signed so she could get him out. We were going to the Brethren Church in Travelers Rest. I think everyone signed the paper. Well, my mother had bought an A-Model Ford after she had picked her cotton and had the money to buy it with.

Well, I was eight-years old now. We were getting ready to go to Columbia. Mama said that we'd have to leave early in the morning. When I laid down, I prayed and said, "Lord, when I shut my eyes, let me awake real quick." He answered my prayer.

Well, we all got ready to leave – Fred and his wife Ellie May, James, Mama, Inez, Christine, Sue, and me. We got down there and we walked up to the governor's capital. Mama handed him the governor the paper she brought. He read them and gave all us children a flag. He had them call down to the jail and had Mr. Stockton come up. The governor told us to march down the steps with our flags held high, so we did. Daddy was going home.

Well, when we got home, Daddy made us work harder than Mama did. Daddy begin to beg Mama to sell the car, but she wouldn't. One day, he started walking down the road. We caught up with him and he said he was going back to Columbia. So Mama gave in for him and sold the car. Daddy saw Mr. Lee Silvers and they went to Gray Court, SC and Mr. Silvers bought some timber. Daddy and Mr. Silvers took slabs down there where they bought the timber and made a cabin. They made a chimney. They made three slab beds and Mama sewed sheets together. She made a slit in the top sheet and stuffed it with straw and that was where we slept, on straw beds. I remember Mama cooking biscuits and frying salmon patties and she would make gravy. Boy, you talking about good eating. It was some of the best.

One day, Inez and Christine and me were out playing in the

woods and we came across a turkey. We went and told Daddy to come and look at the turkey. When he saw it, he told us it was a buzzard. There was something wrong with it. Boy, it sure did smell.

We went to school a while. One day, we went with Mama in the field and there was a peach tree and poison ivy was all over it. Mama said it wouldn't get on her, so she climbed up the peach tree and picked the peaches and slid back down the tree. She got poison ivy all over her.

Daddy and them cut a tree down and it had small squirrels in a nest. He brought them home and we tried to get them to nurse the bottle, but they wouldn't, so they died. Inez, Christine, and me took the squirrels and put them in a match box. We went up on the clay hill and had a funeral for them.

Daddy and Mr. Silvers went up to Glassy Mountain and bought a boundry of timber. When we got up there, they built a barn for the horses and they had one steer and they logged with the steer.

Mama cooked for the saw mill hands. Mr. Silvers told my mother she should can some gravy. Everything she would cook was good. Us kids would get out and make a play house. We would get moss and old broke dishes and make out like we were eating. We had a good time. We would go up to the Boy Scout camp and crawled under the door to the bathroom. We had to use outside bathrooms. Then we went out to where they swam and they would throw beads in the water. When they left to go home, they let the water out. We would go get in the pond and get the beads and we caught bull frogs and took them to Daddy and Mama cooked them. We went back up to the scout camp and we found some butterflies. There sure was a lot of them.

We were eating supper and, one night, a mad dog ran in the house under the table. Daddy told us to get on the table and he shot the dog.

One day, Daddy and Mr. Silvers went to Greenville. Mama went to where us kids were playing and Inez and Ida Sue, my baby sister, got up on the barn. My baby sister fell in the stall and broke her arm. Daddy and Mama were gone all day. When they came home, they had to take her to the doctor and have her arm set. The timber was all cut. We left Glassy Mountain and went to River Falls to cut timber. They rented an old hotel. It was old and no one lived in it anymore. So Mr. Laws rented it to Daddy. It wasn't too good. Daddy, James, Red Ledford, and Uncle Charlie Laws cut timber. We heard about Mr. Henry Jones, and we went to visit them and there were some boys and girls. One girl was married. Helena and Louellen were still at home. We started going up there. Mr. and Mrs. Jones liked to fish and dig for maypop roots, gensing, and blood roots. They had a cabin way up on the mountain. They would go up there and pick huckleberries and go down the street and catch trout. My brother James fell in love with Louellen and they got married.

One day, me, Christine, Ineze, and Ida Sue slipped and got some of Daddy's tobacco. We went under an old house. It had a high porch and we rolled a cigarette and tried to smoke. We started back to the house. We was running. Ineze and Christine and Sue got in front of me and there was a big log in front of me. The Lord spoke to me. He told me I was going to fall. When I got to the log, I fell and it knocked the breath out of me. I finally caught my breath. That was the first time God ever spoke to me. I was nine-years old.

One day, Daddy was riding in the log truck and Mama was walking up the road. Daddy had a woman sitting on his lap. When she got home, she told Mr. Laws and he said, "Come in. When he comes and knocks on the door, you all get under the bed till he leaves." When he left, Mr. Laws took us down to Uncle Jess Batson and he put our things in the corn crib. They set our bed up and the mule stuck his head through the window. The mule would eat corn on our bed. My Aunt Ida, Mama's sister, had a six room house and her and her husband and Lee Neely was all that was in the house. Well, we stayed in the crib till Uncle Jess Batson built us a little shack out at the edge of the woods. Mama would hoe cotton and corn, then when cotton come in, we would pick cotton. Mama was cleaning the yard one day and rolled the cotton cutter on her leg and cut a great big place.

Us girls were small, but we picked cotton right beside Mama.

We would work hard all day and come home and get ready for church. One night, we come home from church and my baby sister wanted to stay all night with Aunt Lola. Mama told her she could not say. Mama picked up a corn stalk and gave her a whippin' with it.

After we moved in the house Uncle Jess made, I remember Mama put gum drops up in the attic for Christmas and I slipped in and got in them. When Christmas would come, sometimes we would get a balloon blown up. We also might get an orange, banana, and an apple and Mama would bake a cake.

One night we went to church and came home and Daddy was sitting on the front porch. He had been gone about a year or more. Well, he went and rented a house from Mr. Duncan, and he planted cotton. I guess around eleven acres and a big bottom of corn. He had to plow with the mules where the corn was. We had muskrats as big as coons. When it rained, the grass would get so thick till we would have to get down and pull the grass from around the corn. Mr. Duncan had a big rooster and it would spur you if he could slip up on you. So Mama said one day, "I'll fix him." She went by there one morning when he run out to spur her and she cut his head off. That old rooster didn't spur no one else.

At the end of the day, when all the work was over, Mama would tell us girls to sing. There was four of us. I was ten-years old. There was Ida Sue, Christine, and Ineze. We didn't have music. We just sang sometimes. We would go up to North Carolina to sing. For Uncle Jess to run a revival one time, we stayed nearly a week. When the crops were over, Daddy rented a house on the McCall's place on White Horse road in Travelers Rest. This was the house I had been born in. Dr. Stanley come to deliver me. I weighed eleven and a half pounds. My mother sure was proud of us children.

Well, we finally got moved from Mr. Duncan's place. We moved down at McCall's place. We had wheat, cotton, corn, potatoes, sweet potatoes, a big garden chicken, and two big hogs. Daddy built a big barn, a cow stall, two stalls for the mules, and a feed room and a big pig pen and a loft. I remember us kids would get green apples and salt and go up in the loft and eat them. Mama had to wash clothes at the wash place. She had a big black pot and three big wood tubs and a plank to stand on. She would boil the white clothes. She would put overalls on a big stump and use a battling stick. She would beat them. That helped get the dirt out of them.

I had to carry water from the spring. Daddy planted wheat and we went behind him and tied it in bundles. Then the men would come and thrash the wheat to take to the mill to make flour. Daddy would put a layer of pine needles, then a layer of sweet potatoes. He done this and then he put dirt around it, then he put corn stalks all the way around it. But he would leave the top open. Then he would build a top over them. We had potatoes all winter.

Come time to gather corn, Daddy would go ahead of us and cut the tops off corn stalks. We would go behind him, stripping the blades of the stalk. We would tie it in bundles and where the top was cut, we would put the fodder over the top. It would dry and then Daddy would gather it and put it in the barn to feed the cows and mules. When the corn got dry, we would gather it and put it in the crib for winter. Daddy would kill the two big hogs and Mama would make two pig pots of lard for the winter. She would make liver pudding and render the lard and make cracklins. Then she made cracklin bread. We moved the next year to Renfrew, and we moved from Renfrew to Slater. Mama and Daddy went to work in the mill. We didn't have to work as hard as we did on the farm, but we had a wonderful time. The Lord gave me a wonderful family and I thank Him.

Now, by this time, I was thirteen-years old. We had moved to Slater. Daddy had bought a house on the mill hill. The mill was in Slater-Marietta, SC and Mama and Daddy and Ineze and Christine went to work at the mill. My mother made a beautiful flower garden. Me and Daddy made a flower bed in an old fish pond that was in the front yard. Daddy worked for a while cleaning looms and oiling them. I guess I worked about one year. Mama kept working and the two girls and my first cousin came to stay with us. Her name was Lora Bayne. She worked in the mill with Mama. They filled batteries. Me and Ida Sue went to school in the old school at Slater-Marietta. They got a new school now. There is a Church of Christ in the old school.

Mama was a wonderful cook. She would fry cabbage and I would go across the street and get our friend. She would come and eat with us. Her name was Lila Cashion. Her husband's name was Emerson Cashion. They had a pretty large family. I stayed some with her at night. Mr. Cashion worked on third. He was a boss man at Slater Mill. Mama would take an eight-pound lard bucket and put ice and salt in a dish pan and she put milk and sugar and peaches in the ice cream bucket. She would shake it with the handles. We had to wash clothes by boiling them in a wash pot, but we had bathrooms. We didn't really know how to act hardly. We went to the Slater Church of God. I always liked to sing in the choir. Me and my three sisters sang, but we didn't have any music. We sure did have a good time. By this time, Daddy came back home and stayed for a while.

My oldest sister was dating B. D. Cash from Georgia. One evening we decided to go visit B. D.'s sister. We walked to her house. She lived on Gayley Mill Road. They lived off the road a piece. Night come and we heard the old hen that was under a chicken pen. The old hen had some diffies. We went out to see what was the matter and there was a black snake under the pen. She got a hoe and killed the snake.

We went back in the house and Mary wanted to show us her brother's picture. He was going to get married over in Australia. When I saw the picture, the Spirit of the Lord spake through me and said that he was mine. Well, I had never seen him before. Mary moved down the road just right out of Marietta, SC. We went to Mary's house one Sunday evening. I had just turned fourteen. When we got there, her brother had come home on furlo. He was sitting just inside the door. He never did say anything. B.D., his brother, had come to see my sister. We had to leave and B.D. said we could ride with him and Ineze. The car was one-seated, so I had to sit in his lap. I'm sure I was scared. I knew if Mama would see me sitting in a boy's lap, I sure would get a tanning because that is something young folks didn't do. We got home and she didn't see me. I sure was glad.

When B.D. come home on leave, he would come to see Inez. Hubert come with him. They both come home on leave at the same time.

That Christmas, they bought us a vanity set for all four of us girls; boy, it sure was pretty. They come every night as long as they were on leave. Well, B.D. and Inez got married around the first of January 1946. Hubert kept coming. I didn't know whether he was coming to see me or my sister. We started to church one evening and I was walking ahead of him. He told me to wait up. I knew he was coming to see me.

Daddy and my youngest brother decided to go to Oregon. I really want Hubert to marry me, but I just turned fifteen so I had to go with them. So Hubert took my little dog and went to Georgia and left the dog with B.D. And Inez.

We left going to Oregon. There were ten of us in the car. We rode three thousand, three hundred miles. I remember us stopping way out there. Some place I didn't know. But we drove up in the yard and they came out and told us to come in. They gave us something to eat. Then we got on the road again. As far as you could see there was nothing but sage brush. We stopped to get us some water. I don't know what was in the water, but you could hardly drink it. I guess we just wasn't used to it.

We got way out there and we stopped to eat at a cafe that was in a trunk of a tree. It was the biggest tree I had ever seen. The cafe was in the truck of the tree and the tree was still thriving. The name of the timber was Redwood. We went on and got our groceries and went down to Newport Logging Camp. Daddy rented a cabin and we began to clean and here come a chipmunk. I jumped up on the bed. I thought it was coming after me. Daddy got a job cutting timber.

One night, we could hear coyotes howling. It sounded like fifty or more. There were mountain lions and there were mule-tail deer. There were big as a cow nearby. There were big, big herds. They had a church right down the road. Me and Ida Sue went down there. There were some friends. There was Norman Parish and Edith, his sister. Daddy and James killed a deer one night and

Mama cured the meat. Daddy cut a ham of the deer and one slice was as big as a platter. Me and Sue went to school out there for a while. I finally quit school. One day, me and Mama and Betty Murdock went to buy groceries. There was a herd of deer. Betty left the road and started up the hill after the deer. But the deer just ran into the bushes. I don't know why she thought she could run them down. We sure did have a good time.

Mama and Daddy went to another town looking for work. They got another job, so we moved down there. We were there for a while and there were three big mountains right up above us. There come word that they were meeting and said for everybody to put their cars across the bridge. About midnight, the water come down the mountain and washed the bridge away. We went across on the swinging bridge.

After that we came back to South Carolina. My boyfriend arrived in Oregan that evening after we had left. He said he was asked to stay, but he caught a bus back home. He got home on a Saturday and asked me if I wanted to go to Georgia with him on Monday. I said yes. So we got married the thirty-first day of December in 1946.

This is my childhood story as good as I can remember.

Part Two

My Experiences

EXPERIENCES IN MINISTRY AND IN HEALING

While he spake these things unto them, behold, there came a certain ruler, and worshipped him, saying, My daughter is even now dead: but come and lay thy hand upon her, and she shall live.

MATTHEW 9:18

My brother's boy, twenty-one years old, had the mind of a six-year old child. They came to our house to visit and as they started to leave, I said to the boy, "Jimmy, tell Uncle Hubert to pray for you." So after he prayed for him, they went on home. They lived down at Fork Shoals, SC. Within a week, they called us and said that Jimmy was helping put a chain link fence up.

Praise God! The Lord Healed Him! All Honor And Glory Belongs To God.

My brother lived in Fork Shoals, SC and my sister-in-law called on a Wednesday for us to come down to their home. She said my brother had a headache and they couldn't get it to stop. They took him to the doctor, but it wouldn't stop hurting. When we got there, the house was full of people. I didn't know what to do. Well, the Lord put it on my heart to read some out of the Bible, and the Holy Ghost spoke through me and said, "If you get saved, I will heal you." He got saved that day, and the Lord healed him. There was five people got saved that day.

Praise God! Give All Glory To God! 1968

And Jesus went about all the cities and villages, teaching in their synagogues, and preaching the gospel of the Kingdom, and healing every sickness and every disease among the people.

MATTHEW 9:35

My brother's youngest son was playing in the yard and my brother had a two-ton truck. He didn't know the boy was behind the truck and he backed up and ran over him. They took him to the doctor. The boy's arm was broke with the bone was sticking out of his arm. The doctor said he'd have to cut his arm off. They came up to our house to visit us. When they started to leave, I said to him, "Randy, have Uncle Hubert pray for you." So we prayed for him and they went home. The next week, Randy called me and told me he was playing ball. The Lord had healed his arm.

Amen! Give God The Glory, For He Is Worthy.

My mother took very ill and couldn't stand for anyone to come into her room. Well, I said to myself, "I know if I write Brother Oral Roberts and send for a prayer cloth that the Lord will heal her." Praise God! So I wrote Bother Oral Roberts and asked him to send me a prayer cloth. I just couldn't wait until I got the prayer cloth. I knew when I got the prayer cloth that God would heal my mother. When I got the prayer cloth, I just could hardly wait until I could get down there to pray. When I got there, I just laid the prayer cloth on her and prayed for her. She told me three days after that prayer, she heard her front door open, and the Lord came in. She said she looked over at the wall of the trailer and saw the Lord pass by. She said it looked like a moving picture show on the wall of the trailer. In three days, she was healed. Jesus passed by!

Praise God And Hallelujah! To God Be All The Glory And Praise And Honor, Amen!

So Jesus had compassion on them and touched their eyes: and immediately their eyes received sight, and they followed him.

MATTHEW 20:34

Daddy and Mama had a prayer meeting at their house. Brother Fields Masters preached that night. When prayer meeting was over, Daddy was sitting at the table. Mama had baked a cobbler pie. He reached across the table and began to move slower and slower. The Lord impressed on me to tell him to ask the Lord to save him. Daddy told me all he knew to do was to just believe on the Lord. We were praying for him and the Spirit of the Lord moved upon my husband to pray for him. When he did, God cast the devil out of him. Daddy couldn't even walk; they had to drag him to the couch. My brother's boy called EMS, but Daddy soon came to himself. He told them there was nothing wrong with Him. God had just cast the devil out of him and saved him.

Praise God! To God Be The Glory And Honor!

When Larry Center was a baby, his mother and daddy brought him to our home. At this time, I had just had some tests done and was in the bed. They brought the baby and laid him on my bed to show me his feet were upside down. (The bottom of his feet was on the top and the top of his feet were on the bottom.) After we prayed for him, they went home. We received a call one day that God had healed his feet! He is grown and working for the Lord, singing and playing instruments.

I Thank You Lord. I Give You Honor And Praise For Everything!

After that He put His hands again upon His eyes and made him look up: and he was restored, and saw every man clearly.

MARK 8:25

We lived down below Old Hilltop Church on Highway 25 in a house. There was an old dog come to our house. She had caught a rabbit and laid it down at my husband's feet. One day, she came home and she couldn't see out of one of her eyes. The Lord impressed me to go and get a wet wash rag and wipe her eyes and pray for her. After that, she began to take her paw and rub her eyes. You knew God healed that old dog's eyes and after that she could see.

Amen! All Honor To God! Praise God For Everything!

My baby daughter, Ruth Ann, comes to see me one day and she showed me a mole on her. So I prayed just a simple prayer like I always do. The next time I saw her, she said she had looked one day and the mole was gone. It just fell off. The Lord healed her.

Amen!

Isn't God So Good? Give God The Glory! Praise God!

And a woman having an issue of blood twelve years which had spent all her living upon physicians, neither could be healed of any, came behind Him, and touched the border of His garment: and immediately her issue of blood stanched.

LUKE 8: 43,44

My mother had surgery on her bladder; it needed fixing. After she came home, the place where she had had surgery came wide open. When I went to her bed and saw where the incision had come open, I just couldn't touch her. I told her I'd be back in a little while. We had a prayer rock down in the woods where we would go pray. That day I went down to the prayer rock. I didn't even go down the path; I cut through the woods. I fell down on my knees and started praying. I prayed and prayed. I started back up to the house and I could not stop crying. I would lean against a tree and then I could go a little further. And again I did the same thing. I couldn't take care of her for a week; my sister had to take care of her. After a week went by, I started taking care of her again. I had to take and swab out the wound to clean it, three times a day. One night, the Lord showed me the wound was healed. The devil tried to make me doubt, but I knew inside me that the Lord was going to heal her. On Monday, my husband and I had to go somewhere. On Tuesday, my sister came and took care of her. On Wednesday, when my sister came back to change and clean the wound, it was healed. She told Mama that the wound was healed. My mother asked for a mirror to see and she could see that the Lord had worked an amazing miracle on her. She went back to the doctor and told him that God had healed her. The doctor said to give him a little praise and credit, but she knew the Lord had healed her.

All Honor, Glory, And Praise Is Given To Our Lord And Savior Jesus Christ!

My husband and I went to see our granddaughter Carol. It was up in the middle of the day. Carol told me to look at this knot on her foot. I said, let us pray. Well, we just said a simple prayer. After that, she was sitting on my husband's lap one day and looked down at her foot and saw that the knot was gone. God had wonderfully healed her. He's the One that has done all these miracles!

Give Glory To God!

And they departed, and went through the towns, preaching the gospel, and healing every where.

LUKE 9:6

We were all invited to a homecoming at my cousin's house. All of the family and friends went. We had singing and then dinner. I had went in the house and Mrs. Turner couldn't walk. I asked her if she wanted prayer. I went with her and her daughter in the back room. There was another lady that joined us. When we started to pray, the other lady went out. We continued to pray and she said that it felt like electricity jumping all over her. Right then and there, God wonderfully healed her. That was so wonderful!

To God Be All The Honor, Glory, And Praise! What A Mighty God We Serve!

My great grandson, William, was maybe three or four and there was a knot come up on the back of his leg, right behind his knee. He had a doctor's appointment to have it checked. We prayed for him and a few days after, the knot was gone. Dora Ann went ahead and took him to the doctor, and the doctor said he didn't know what it could've been. But we told the doctor that God healed it, but he said it probably went away by itself. We know God healed it. That's why it went away.

Amen! Praise The Lord! Thank You For Healing!

My oldest son, Clyde, had measles when he was young. He got up too early and the measles fell on him in one of this lungs. He had a spot as big as a quarter on this lung. Brother Duncan anointed and prayed for him and God healed him.

Give God The Honor And Glory!

And it came to pass on a certain day, as He was teaching, that there were Pharisees and doctors of the law sitting by, which were come out of every town of Galilee, and Judea, and Jerusalem: and the power of the Lord was present to heal them.

LUKE 5:17

I, my husband, and my first cousin had gone to church. We had just got home when my cousin called and said there was a lady down there that needed prayer. This lady had fixed an apple pie and as she was getting it out of the oven, she spilled it on her hand and it blistered up. When we got down there, we anointed and prayed for her hand. Afterward, we were just standing there talking and she began to say, "Look! It's getting well." God worked a miracle right there. Praise God! Also, this same lady had lost two or three babies and wanted us to pray that she would be able to carry the next baby. We heard from her later, and she told us she was able to carry the next baby. Praise God!

Isn't God Good? All Honor And Praise To Our Lord And Savior! Amen!

My middle daughter, Flora Jean, had a toothache and she also had sugar diabetes. She said, "Mama, will you pray for me?" So I anointed her and just said a simple prayer. The next morning, when she got up, she said, "I believe God healed my sugar diabctcs." Notice what she said. "I believe God healed my sugar diabetes." Just a simple faith. So I took her back to the doctor and the doctor said she no longer had sugar diabetes. So see, God not only healed her toothache, but the sugar diabetes also.

Praise God! Give God All The Glory And Honor!

And Jesus went about all Galilee, teaching in their synagogues and preaching the gospel of the Kingdom and healing all manner of sickness and all manner of disease among the people.

MATTHEW 4:23

And behold, there was a woman which had a spirit of infirmity eighteen years, and was bowed together, and could in no wise lift up herself. And when Jesus saw her, He called her unto Him, and said unto her, woman, thou art loosed from thine infirmity. And he laid His hands on her: and immediately she was made straight, and glorified God.

LUKE 13:11-13

My husband, Hubert, had to go to the V.A. in Asheville. He said that when he started back, he remember leaving the V.A. and coming back down the road until he got to the sign that said Greenville. He said he didn't remember anything else until he came to himself and he was going toward Spartanburg. There were big trucks passing by him and it really scared him. We believe the Spirit of God must have been driving the car or else he would have wrecked and there's no telling what might have happened.

Praise God! There's Nothing God Can't Do!

I had a mole on my right shoulder. One day it began to itch and water was around the outside of the mole. The family kept saying you need to go to the doctor and let them see what it is. So I finally gave in and went to see the doctor. The doctor said the mole was deep in there, so he sent me to a cancer doctor. Doris Ann, my oldest daughter, took me. The doctor told me I would have to have surgery. They found out it was melanoma cancer and I would have to have another surgery and take chemo treatments. I had all the church praying for me that I wouldn't have to take the treatments. I went down so they could draw blood. Then I went back to see the doctor and to start chemo treatments. The doctor came in and then said, "Wait, I'll be back in a minute." He came back in and told me that I wouldn't have to take the treatments. Thank God! I went home and my cousin's daughter and her mom came. She said the Lord put it on her heart to come and pray for me; so they prayed for me. We were going to church at Cleveland Church of God at the time and when I got back to church, Brother R. L. Case anointed and prayed for me. I felt something like the electricity go under my right arm. That is when the Lord healed me. Amen! I've been healed going on twenty-one years.

Thank God For Healing Me.

Jesus saith unto him, if thous canst believe, all things are possible to him that believeth.

MARK 9:23

The Lord sent me back one morning after the children left for school. I had laid back down to rest a little bit longer. I had shut my eyes and there appeared a great big light before me. Immediately, I went to this place where I was sitting in a rocking chair and there were a lot of people around me. There appeared a dove and one of its eyes was white and one was pink. Then another dove came and it sat on my finger. It talked to me in the Holy Ghost. After this, there were three angels stood before me and said, "The Father has a favor to ask of you." They said, "We'll have to wait until it gets dark." They took my hands and we ran as fast as we could. We stood on top of the mountain, and then I saw the prettiest hedge row I had ever seen. Then I mentioned my hands were getting cold and immediately I was standing before God's giant big hands. The angels said, "We could have brought her dead, but we brought her as she was." I didn't see anything but His giant big hands. In His hands, He was working something and it was gray in color. He took and broke a piece off, handed it to me, and told me to take it and eat it and go back and wait until He called for me. I give God the glory and honor for letting me be here today, witnessing and working for Him. I'm still waiting for him to call me home.

Praise God! All Honor Is Due To God!

My oldest daughter, Doris Ann, was playing in the front yard in the sand. She had started crying. I knew something was wrong. I went to the door and her eyes were full of sand. I said, "Lord, let this sand all be gone when I'm finished praying." So when I finished praying, the sand was all gone. This was the first miracle the Lord let me see.

Thank God! I Give God The Honor And Glory.

And when He had looked round about on them with anger, being grieved for the hardness of their hearts, He saith until the man, Stretch forth thine hand. And he stretched it out: and his hand was restored whole as the other.

MARK 3:5

One time I had a hurting in my left arm. It would get better and then it would start hurting again. It had done this about two years. We moved to Marietta, and, one day, I went to walk my dog. I was praying and I told the Lord, "Lord, you just have to help me." The Holy Ghost came down and hit me so hard that I almost fell to the ground. Well, it was a night or so later, and I had a vision of me and my granddaughter, Carol. We were in this old house. We looked out across the pasture and it looked like a bear and a man coming toward us. Carol and I ran out the front door. She kept on running, but I went back. I realized that it wasn't a bear, but a man. When he came out of the house, he had on an army suit. He caught up with me and laid his hand on my left shoulder and said, "I'll break the yoke off of you."

Praise God! He Sent An Angel In The Night And Healed Me.

I Give God All The Praise!

We went to pick blackberries one day. It was me and my two sons, Clyde and Robert. As we stepped up into the berry patch, I said, "Lord, don't let a snake bite us." As we walked out in the field, there was a bunch of sage brush and it began to move. The devil told me to stomp it and that it might be a rabbit or a rat. But there was something that wouldn't let me. Just about then, there was a snake rose up out of the grass and it stood as tall as me, but there was a shield between me and the snake. I thank God He took care of us.

Praise God!

And He put forth his hand, and touched him, saying, I will: be thou clean. And immediately the leprosy departed from him.

LUKE 5:13

Della Foster's youngest girl had asthma real bad. She was maybe seven or eight years old, I think. On this one morning, she had a real bad asthma attack. Well, Della was going to come over to our house for prayer, but she didn't know how to get there. Anyway, she stepped out on faith and started to drive the car. She said something took hold of the wheel of the car and brought her right to our house. When they got there, I went out to meet them. The little girl could hardly breathe. I laid my hands on her and said a simple prayer and she was instantly healed.

Praise God For Everything! Give God The Glory!

The Spirit Of God Can Drive A Car! Praise God!

My brother James, his wife, and I went down to Greenwood to fish. While we were there, we got a phone call that my oldest son Clyde had an accident at the river. He had gone swimming, and, when he dove in the water, he hit a rock. He had broken his neck, so we hurried to the hospital. He stayed there for a month. I would stay with him through the week and his wife would stay on the weekends. We stayed day and night. I slept on a porch-type lounge chair. One day, I looked at the wall and I saw an angel. I would look down and back to the wall and the angel was still there. The angel stayed there on the wall in his room. Shortly after this happened, the doctor came in. By this time, Clyde had gotten better. The doctor said, "Son, it wasn't me that made you better." God had performed a miracle right there in that hospital.

Praise God For His Miracles!

And behold, a woman, which was diseased with an issue of blood twelve years, came behind Him, and touched the hem of His garment:

MATTHEW 9:20

One time I was staying with this lady. Her name was Mrs. Willis. She was in her nineties. They had called Mr. Bryant to come and fix her well pump. He was out there trying to fix something on the well pump with a screw driver; it slipped and hit right about his thumb and cut it. When he came in, I asked him if he wanted us to pray for him. He said yes. When we laid our hands on him and prayed for him, he hit the floor like a bullet. When he got up, he said, "I believe the prayer helped." He went on home and they took him to the emergency room. The doctor said the blood vessel in his thumb was cut in two, but it wasn't even bleeding. My grand-daughter and I saw Mr. and Mrs. Bryant as Hardees, and he told us what the doctor had said. Mr. Bryant said it didn't even leave a scar.

Now That Was A Miracle. Give God The Glory! Praise God!

God Is All powerful, And Oh, What Power He Has!

We were having revival at the little church on Chestnut Ridge Road in Marietta where I was preaching the Word of God. There was a little girl that had braces on her legs and they were spread out as far as they could go. That's the way she had to walk. Her name was Teresa Green. All that week I prayed for her, and my prayers were that when she went back to the doctor that her legs would be healed. So when she went back to the doctor, the braces were taken off and she was healed by God. Give God the glory! In the same revival, there was one night when the church was full. When I got done preaching, I had sat down and I got very sick. I could not hardly stand it. So I stood up and asked if there was someone there that was very sick and could hardly stand it. There was a girl that stood up. I told her that if she would come up, the Lord would heal her. She was instantly healed. She told me thank you, but I told her that it wasn't me and that she needed to thank God and give Him the glory. Is there anything too hard for God? No! There is nothing too hard for God.

Praise God For Everything!

And Jesus rebuked him, saying, hold thy peace, and come out of him.
MARK 1:25

There was one time I was called to go preach at this church in Mauldin. The preacher there had one arm. We were getting ready to go and I was fixing my hair. I felt led by the Spirit of the Lord to go to the front door, so I went and, as I got to the front door, there was something that began to wiggle under my feet. It was a snake. Then it ran out from under my feet and, when it did, it raised up nearly as high as I was. I called for my husband, Hubert, and told him there was a snake in the house. He ran outside to get an ax so he could cut its head off. Once he cut its head off, he took and threw it outside. Shortly, after, he went back outside to check on it and it was gone. Well, we went on to church! The service began and we got up to sing. It was very hard to sing. The preacher said to have a Glory Land March. As we were marching around, there was the woman and when I passed by her, she said, "I love you." Then she stood up and said, "The devil tells me I'm not saved." After that, I got up to preach and, unlike other times, I had to read straight from the Bible. When I got through reading, I gave an altar call. There was a young boy come down and gave his heart to God. This same woman I spoke of earlier stood up and said, "The devil tries to tell me I'm not saved." She came to the altar and the saints began to pray for her. While they were praying for her, I tried to sing I Saw the Light, but I just could not sing it. I laid my accordion down and went to help the preacher pray for that woman. She fell back to the floor. We knelt down to continue to pray for her. The preacher had his one hand on her head. The Lord impressed upon me to put my hand on her stomach, and, when I did, the devil began to come out of her. The woman was wiggling back and forth just like that snake had done under my feet before leaving home that evening. Well, it wasn't long after this took place that the preacher's wife shot his head off. She went to prison, but I'm not sure how long she had to stay. When the devil comes out of someone, he's going to find somewhere to go and this shows where he went. Thank God for deliverance. To God be the glory for everything.

We Can't Thank Him Enough For Everything He Has Allowed Us To Experience.

When Jesus saw their faith, He said unto the sick of the palsy, Son, they sins be forgiven thee.

MARK 2:5

My good friend Maye Serrett came to see me one day. She had cancer on her face about the size of a half dollar. We got to praying and God's presence filled the room. She said it felt like worms crawling in her face, but Jesus came and healed her that day.

We Give God The Glory For Everything.

We had a friend name Dave Frazier who was also our uncle. When I was small, Mrs. Frazier said that I was her daughter. After, I was married and had children, we went by to see them one day. Uncle Dave had gone to feed his chickens. He had a wart on his arm, right below his shoulder and a hen had pecked it off. Well, he would not go to the doctor. The family tried to get him to go, but he just would not go. His arm was so bad it looked like it would rot off. It was like that for seven years. One day, my husband, my mother, Lucille Hall, and I went by there and we prayed for him. After that, we heard in a few days from them and they told us that his arm was healed.

Praise God!

There also came a multitude out of the cities round about unto Jerusalem, bringing sick folks, and them which were vexed with unclean spirits: and they were healed every one.

ACTS 5:16

And by the hands of the apostles were many signs and wonders wrought among the people; (and they were all with one accord in Solomon's Porch.

ACTS 5:12

It was November 19, 2004, and my husband Hubert, my oldest son Clyde, and I had to go down to the Greenville V.A. When we were coming back, I came back through West Greenville by Woodside Mill. We came to where the mill was. There was a car cut right across in front of us and we t-boned the other car. Clyde, who was in the front seat, hit the dash so hard it broke. Hubert hit the back seat because neither seatbelt worked. EMS was called and they took us to the hospital. We waited to be seen for five hours. There was this woman doctor who came in. She asked, "Why haven't these people who were in an accident been seen?" Finally they took us back to be checked and found out that Hubert had cracked his sternum and broke three ribs. Clyde was checked out. They said there was nothing wrong with him, so they sent him home. I was fine. About three weeks later, Clyde got very sick. He was sick all night. The next morning, he called me. My daughter Doris Ann took him down to North Greenville Emergency Room in Travelers Rest. We got down there and I called for a wheel chair. They came and started to take him out of the car and he went into a coma. They thought he was taking drugs, but we told them about the accident that we were in three weeks earlier. After this, Clyde started jerking all over and gritting his teeth; he was having a seizure. So they took him back for an x-ray and found out he was in real bad shape. He was transported to Greenville Memorial Hospital. When he got there, they did a heart cather and a cat-scan on him. It showed he had an aneurism in his head. They had to put a hole in his head to drain the blood off his brain. He stayed unconscious, but the doctors said his chances were gray, meaning it didn't look like he would recover. There were a lot of people praying for him. I was in there with him one day and he said to me somebody passed by my bed. He said, "I see a gate over yonder." I asked him if he wanted to be saved and he did. That day, he gave his heart to God. So, you see, Jesus had passed by his bed that day. After that, he began to get better. Soon after, they sent him down to Roger C. Peace for therapy, and he stayed there about a month. After that, he was taken to the Bryan Center in North Carolina and he stayed there about seven months. Then he got well enough to come home. Today, he is still living for God and goes to church with us.

Praise God! Give God The Glory For Everything!

And Peter said unto him, Aeneas, Jesus Christ maketh thee whole: arise, and make thy bed. And he arose immediately.

ACTS 9:34

I was in the hospital having some tests done. There was a black lady there and she was very ill. She had bowel trouble and she couldn't get strength because it drained all the fluids out of her body. Well, for a week I would talk to her and help her. I knew I had to win her confidence in order to win her soul to Jesus Christ. At this particular time, when I felt impressed from the Lord to talk with her about salvation, she had went to the bathroom. So I went in there and asked her if she was saved. She said no. I asked her if she wanted to be saved, and she said yes. So we prayed right there and she received Jesus Christ as her personal savior. It doesn't matter where you're at, God will save you.

Amen! Give God The Glory For Everything!

My husband and I went to see Mrs. Peace. When we got there, she was sitting with her leg elevated. Her leg was swollen, so we anointed and prayed for her leg. The next time we heard from her, God had healed her leg.

Give God Glory For Everything!

How God anointed Jesus of Nazareth with the Holy Chost and with power: who went about doing good, and healing all that were oppressed of the devil; for God was with Him.

ACTS 10:38

Brother Duncan, Hubert, and I went to Terry Creek Holiness Pentecostal Church on Highway 25. There was a man there that the people wanted us to pray for. When we got there, the man was sitting on the front porch. We went out on the porch to pray for him, but the man said, "You are not going lay your hands on my head." Brother Duncan tried to put his hand on his head, but his hand would just slide off. He tried again but the devil spoke through the man again and refused to let him lay hands on his head. So you see, the man did not want deliverance, and if a person doesn't want deliverance, he will not get it. We knew that God was there to deliver and set him free, but he didn't want to be delivered and set free. We went and done what God wanted us to do, but the man just didn't want to be delivered and set free. His blood is off our hands. What would a man give in exchange for his soul?

We Give God The Glory For Everything! Praise The Lord God!

There was another time that Brother Duncan, my husband, and I were called to go pray for a man that had a stroke. Brother Duncan told us that when we got there and prayed for this man, that when we started to leave, we should not look back. Well, we got ready to leave and the devil told my husband to look back, and he did. When he did, he was half way paralyzed. For one whole week, he was like that. So we learned a lesson from disobeying what the lord said through Brother Duncan. From that time, we always reverenced the Lord and do what he says when anyone is prayed for.

Give God The Glory For Everything!

But my God shall supply all your needs according to his riches in glory by Christ Jesus.

PHILIPPIANS 4:19

We lived in O'Neal, SC, and we went to the Pentecostal Church of God there. Brother Duncan had preached on healing. He was living under the influence of divine healing for sixty years. He never took even an aspirin. He was a grand preacher and taught us many things. If we had a doubt about anything, we would go and ask him about it because he was a man of God. At this time, we had all five or our children (Doris Ann, Clyde, Robert, Flora Jean, and Ruth Ann). They were all pretty young. We had some neighbors that were in pretty bad shape. She had four children and her husband was in prison. One day, our children were playing with her children and her children told my children that all they had to eat was grits. They asked if they could eat dinner with us. So our children came in and asked me and I said yes. At this time, we didn't have a lot either, so I began to talk to the Lord about it. I knew I didn't have much flour. When I made up the dough, it was about the size of a saucer or maybe a little bit bigger. I told the Lord that I didn't have much bread to feed all of the children. I put the dough in the middle of a biscuit pan and padded it out and baked it. When I got it out, the pan was plum full of bread. It was enough to feed all of us and some left over.

Praise God For Providing!

We lived over on Highway 25. One day after the older children were gone to school and my husband was gone to work, Ruth Ann and I were there at the house. She was about three-years old. I was washing windows and my hand slipped. I cut my finger. I almost fainted when I saw the blood. My little girl begins to pray for me, and she said, "Dear God, heal my Mama. Don't let the devil kill her." God healed me. It quit bleeding. She had that child-like faith.

Praise God! Give God The Glory!

And Jesus answering saith unto them, have faith in God.

MARK 11:22

My husband and I were having prayer meeting down at Fork Shoals. We were going every Saturday night. We had a house full and people were getting saved and filled with the Holy Ghost. One night, there was a man there that had ulcers real bad. We were outside in the yard and the man came up to my husband and said, "God told me that if you will pray for me, He would heal me." At that moment, my husband didn't want to pray for him, so I tried to pray for him, but the Lord wouldn't let me. After that, the man took Hubert's hand and laid it on himself and God instantly healed him. He said after that he went home and ate a hamburger and dill pickles and it didn't hurt him. So, you see, the man had faith in God that God would do what he said if he would obey Him.

Give God The Glory!

Several years ago, one of our daughters got hit and killed by a car. We had her funeral at Howze Mortuary. While we were at the mortuary, the owner at the time was Mr. Towns Howze. He asked me to be his adopted mother and, of course, I said yes. He called me Mama Cash. Mr. Howze got sick and went to the doctor; they said he had cancer of the throat. They did surgery and afterward, gave him radiation. Hubert and I stopped by the mortuary to see how he was. At this time, they lived upstairs at the mortuary. His wife took us upstairs to where he was. He was in bed, and we prayed for him. When we prayed, the healing power of God touched him and healed him.

Give God The Glory And Honor For He Is Worthy!

God Can Do Anything If We Will Have Faith And Believe Him!

And the prayer of faith shall save the sick, and the Lord shall raise him up: and if he have committed sins, they shall be forgiven him.

JAMES 5:15

There was this one time I was called to come and preach on Sunday night. That night, after I got done preaching, I gave an altar call. There was a woman sitting way back in the church. She came up for prayer. She told me later that God spoke to her and said if you will let Mrs. Cash pray for you, you will be healed. This lady had not been able to speak in two years, so I anointed and prayed for her. She started shouting out, "I can talk! I can talk!" God healed her just like He said He would.

Amen! Praise God!

Hubert and I were asked to come and run a revival in Toccoa, Georgia. This man from the Slater Church of God, Brother Self, went with us. The church was packed, the Lord was blessing, and the altar was full. My mother was helping pray around the altar. At this time, it was winter and they heated the church with a gas heater. The heater was pretty close to the altar. There was a lady praying at the altar and she fell out in the Spirit. Her long hair went right into the flames of the heater. She laid there for a while, but, you know, when she got up her hair was not even singed. Oh, how powerful is the power of God! We had a great revival.

Praise God For Everything!

But without faith it is impossible to please him: for he that cometh to God must believe that he is, and that he is a rewarder of them that diligently seek him.

HEBREWS 11:6

46

I was scheduled to have a shoulder replacement surgery. The same week I was going to have the surgery, I went to church and had my pastor pray for me. When she prayed for me, she told me the Lord said not to worry. Everything was going to be alright. Then I began to put self aside and believe in God. On August 3, 2011, I went to the hospital to have my shoulder operated on. When they got ready to take me back to start my procedure, the doctor asked my daughter Ruth Ann if she wanted to go back with me and hold my hand until they were ready to take me into the operating room.

The doctor told us they were going to put a nerve block in my neck. So they started to put the needle in my neck and was putting the medicine in to block the pain. Ruth Ann was holding my hand, praying and telling me not to worry. Then, all at once, my eyes turned the color of blood and I started foaming at the mouth. My heart stopped beating and the doctor and nurses started working to try and get my heart to beat. My daughter was standing by my bedside the whole time. She said she had never prayed so hard in her life. They worked on me for twenty-five minutes, then they finally got my heart to start beating again. I came back to life. The Doctor up above, God, brought me back to life because he still has work for me to do. The doctor that worked on me told me the next day that I was his miracle child.

I can do all things through Christ which stregnthenth me.
PHILIPPIANS 4:13

Rejoice in the Lord always: and again I say, rejoice.
PHILIPPIANS 4:4

My granddaughter, Carol, had a knot on the top part of her foot. I prayed for it and it was healed.

Hubert came to me one day and gave me a flower. He told me that if it hadn't been for my faith and the way I had lived, he would have never made it. You never know the influence you might have.

In the midst of the street of it, and on either side of the river, was there the tree of life, which bare twelve manner of fruits, and yielded her fruit every moth: and the leaves of the tree were for the healing of the nations.

REVELATION 22:2

Part Three

Ministry

A RECORD OF MY MINISTRY AND THE
MESSAGES I PREACHED

During my ministry, I kept a record of the messages I preached as well as when and where I preached them. This may not be all my messages, but it is a good record and representation from my ministry. I want to   do all my God that I might win the lost for God.

(Editor's Note: The following entries show a record of Ruth Cash's preached messages and other works in the ministry. This may not be a comprehensive list. Some entries will have information that other entries do not, such as date, day of the week, or other information. The entries listed below represent the information as listed in her original handwritten journal.)

I preached at Landrum Pentecostal Church of God. On the first night, two testified. My message was on Cain and Able (Genesis 4:23).

Thursday night at Highlands Church of God, my message was The Parable of the Great Supper. (Matthew 22:1-14) The love offering was fifty dollars.

Revival at Terry Creek Pentecostal Holiness Church, 1973. Scripture used: Luke 22, Matthew 26, Mark 14. Peter's Denial of Jesus. "And the Lord said, Simon, Simon, behold, Satan hath desired to have you, that he may sift you as wheat:" (Luke 22:31) The Lord blessed the first night we prayed for the sick.

Terry Creek Pentecostal Holiness Church (1973): Moses and the Burning Bush: Exodus 3 and 4. The plagues the Lord sent to Egypt.

Terry Creek Pentecostal Holiness Church (1973). Acts 10. Attendance was 18. Some got blessed, but no one got saved. Love offering was $15.

On Mother's Day in 1973, I preached at Landrum Pentecostal Church. I preached on the sparrow. Psalm 84:3; Psalm 102:7; Matthew 10:29-31; Luke 12:6.

The last Sunday night in December 1973, I preached at Greenville Pentecostal Mission. One got saved. My message was Lazarus and the rich man. "How shall we escape, if we neglect so great salvation." (Hebrews 2:3). That same morning I taught Sunday School. Matthew 25: 1-46.

1974. A Perfect Heart. David, a man after God's own heart. Acts 13:22. David prayed for his son, King Solomon. (Out of a man's heart and the issues of life.)

1975. My first revival was in December. Deliverance Tabernacle. 2 saved, 4 sanctified, 3 received the Holy Ghost. Thank God. The revival ran Wednesday through Saturday. The offering was $27.

Third week in at Brother Duncan's church. I preached on holiness. 2 got saved, 3 sanctified, and 1 received the Holy Ghost. No offering.

I ran a revival at Brother Duncan's church, Thursday through Sunday night. 2 got healed. The saints were revived. The offering was $33. I gave Brother Duncan $11 out of the offering.

On the last Sunday in February 1975, I preached at Lima Church of God. No one got saved. Offering was $3 and some change.

Sunday night, I preached at Brother Duncan's church and the Lord blessed. No one saved. No offering.

On the first Wednesday night in March, 1975, I preached on the lost sheep, the lost coin, and the Prodigal Son. Another service, I preached on Lazarus being raised from the dead. During a third service, the Holy Ghost took over. 4 were saved and 2 were healed. Thank God.

October 6. Pentecostal Church of God. Walhalla, SC. Wednesday night. I preached on Matthew 5:11 and Matthew 25. 4 were prayed for. Offering was $23.

October 14, 1999. Brother Perry's church. Thursday night. I preached from Matthew 24 and 25. The Lord blessed the service. The offering was $21.23. Praise God!

Thursday night at John Perry's church, I preached on the parable of the sower, Matthew 13. It was sure hard to preach. There were 14 people there. Praise God. He is greater than the devil. The devil is defeated. Praise God! I prayed for 4 people. No offering.

November 19, 1978. I preached at the Cleveland Church of God. I preached from Jeremiah 18. The Potter's House. 2 received the Holy Ghost.

Sunday 1978. November 26. Revival at the Cleveland Church of God. Luke 15. The Prodigal Son. I preached twice. The other preachers were Brother Carter, Brother Perry, and Brother Barry.

Sunday Night, 1978. Jeremiah 18. Cleveland Church of God. 2 received the Holy Ghost.

1978. I preached the last Thursday night in November. I preached on bearing fruit. Luke3:8. John 15:1-8. No offering. Several got blessed. I also preached about banana pudding and fitting the pattern together.

Sunday Night 1978. John 14. We had a wonderful time in the Lord. A woman had been backslid for 15 years and had not felt the Lord. She got saved that night and received the Lord.

1978. Thursday night. Fork Shoals. 1 received the Holy Ghost. 2 sanctified. I preached on John 14. We had a great service. Offering was $18.

1979. Wednesday Night. I was asked to preach at the Cleveland Church of God. There was a brother that wanted to testify. His name was Brother Barry. He was a sandy-haired boy and thin. I got started preaching and preached on the whole armor of God. Ephesians 6. Everyone got blessed. 1 saved. 1 received the Holy Ghost.

January 5, 1979. At my house on a Friday night from 10 pm till 2 am. Some guests came to my house. I started talking about the Lord. One woman got saved, sanctified, and filled with the Holy Ghost. Her daughter also got saved. What a meeting!

January 15, 1979. Brother Bill's Full Gospel Church in Brevard, NC. 2 people preached. No one got saved, but the Lord blessed. Romans 9:10,11. Ephesians 6:10-17. Offering was $12 and change.

January 1979. Cleveland Church of God. Brother Carter went to prayer conference and left the church in charge of me. Brother Barry took charge till time for me to preach. I showed the water and eggs. Roman 9,10,11. Ephesians 6. Revelation 16:17-20. No one saved. No offering.

January 23, 1979, Tuesday night. We had had a meeting at the Greenville MHF nursing home. Brother and Sister Bibby come. He played his horn and testified. I sang and read from John 14. We had a good service.

February 1979. Brevard, NC. First Sunday night of the month. Luke 8:16. Matthew 5:18. We had a blessed time rejoicing in the Lord. The offering was $18 and some change.

February 1979. I preached at Pine Forest, NC on a Thursday night. Luke 8:16. No one saved. Small offering. Brother Cash jumped the bench.

Cleveland Church of God. I preached from Romans 12 and Ephesians 6. No one saved, but God blessed. 2 got anointed. Praise God! No offering.

May 6, 1979. 2 were saved and delivered at my house. Thank God for the souls.

June 1979. Cleveland Church of God. Matthew 7:18. I preached on the fruit. It was a good service. God blessed. No one saved. No offering.

August 8, 1979. Freewill Baptist Church. I preached from Romans 12. 4 saved. 2 sanctified. 1 demon cast out. No offering.

August 22, 1979. Fork Shoals Church of God. We preached on the 10 virgins. 1 saved. First night of a revival. On the second night, I preached on the prodigal son. 2 saved. On the third night, I preached on John 14. 6 saved. A good revival. Offering was $33.50.

August 25, 1979. We had the Lord's Supper at Fork Shoals Church of God.

August 27, 1979. I went to the clinic for Flora Jean. There I met a woman whose baby was sick with a fever. For 24 hours, I was talking about some blessing god had been doing and she heard me. She came to me and said she heard me talking. She said that if her daughter and baby sat down beside of me and I prayed for them, then God would heal the baby. God healed that baby.

August 27, 1979. This happened at my home. Sister Mary went to the doctor. He said she probably had cancer on her face. We came back home. She said it burned and crawled like worms. I got to praying and crying. God instantly healed her.

The sisters of the church went to pray from this sister who had psoriasis on her hand. They were in this shape for 5 year. The women and 2 others prayed for her. The next day, she could wash dishes. She doubted and it came back. She went to Atlanta, Georgia on a Friday and something happened. The nurse was holding her hands and said that something was happening. The scabs fell of her hands and they were completely healed.

August 29, 1979. Revival in Brevard, NC. On the first night, I preached on Matthew 5. 1 sanctified. The grand-girls sang with me. Offering was $11 and some change. During the third night and the fourth night, the Holy Ghost took over. During the revival, 3 saved, 5 sanctified, 4 received Holy Ghost, and 2 healed.

1979. Alice Batson healed at home from arthritis. Praise God!

September 1979. Revival at Brush Harbor, Forestville. God showed me a man in the meeting. He stepped forth. He had a big hole in his right arm. God touched him.

1979. A woman in Greenville had a swelling and could not wear certain shoes. After prayer, God healed her.

1979. My first cousin healed of a heart attack.

1979. Sister Linda came to me house and said God had been dealing with her for 2 or 3 months. She asked God to save her. I believe He did.

1979. Sister Maxine. God healed her kidneys. Praise God.

1980. I was called to go to work at Stroud's Hospital. I cooked for about 5 months. After I worked about a month or so, Lois Gates come to my house and gave her heart to God. What a wonderful family. Thank God!

1980. At Brother Howard's church, the Church of God of Prophecy on Chestnut Ridge Road in Marietta, SC. Lois Gates' brother came to church. After I got through preaching, I asked him if he wanted to give his heart to God and he said yes. Praise God!

1980. I was asked to teach Sunday School. I told them I wasn't a teacher, I was a preacher. I did the best I could. Lois Gates' sister-in-law came and after we got through the lesson, I asked her if she wanted to be saved. She came forth and told of how she saw hell and how she had seen the devil. She said she had even felt the heat of hell. Thank God for another soul saved.

1980. Marietta, SC. I preached on Matthew 22, Luke 14. No one saved, but it was a good meeting. Offering was $19 and some change.

November, 17, 1980. Marietta, SC. Luke 16. We had a good turn out. Thank God! No one saved. Offering was $7.

November 18, 1980. Marietta, SC. Brother Cash testified. I sang 3 or 4 songs, and then I preached on Luke 19. No one saved. Offering was $7 and some change.

November 19, 1980. Marietta, SC. John 14. Some of our children were there. Doris helped me sing. No one saved. Offering was $5.22.

November 20, 1980. Marietta, SC. Luke 15: lost sheep, lost coin, prodigal son. After the service, we had an altar call and everyone came around and prayed. We all sat down. I became so sick I was deathly sick. I asked if any one was sick. A young girl right behind me was so sick. She came up and God healed her right her. She thanked me for healing her, but I told her it was God. A woman was praying. She said she saw Jesus. Of course, she got satisfied. 1 sanctified. 1 healed. Offering was $7.

November 22, 1980. Marietta, SC. The Holy Ghost took over. The small children sang. The preacher turned the service over to me. We sang "Highway to Heaven," and other songs. 1 saved. Offering was $7.

November 23, 1980. Marietta, SC. Luke 19. Genesis 7. We had a good revival. This was the final night. No one saved. No offering.

November 23, 1980. I went to see Mama this Sunday morning. She was upset. We comforted her. I prayed for her. We left around 11:45. We went to another house. We sang some songs and while we were singing another man came. I preached from Luke 19. He gave his heart to God.

December 7, 1980. Brevard, NC. I was scheduled to preach, but the Holy Ghost took over. 1 received the Holy Ghost. Offering was $23 and some change.

December 13, 1980. We went to see Mama in the nursing home. I went down the hall and got one of our colored friends. I brought her to Mama's room. I talked about Luke 18 and 19. We had prayer and a good time.

December 14, 1980. Brevard, NC. I preached on Luke 18 and 19. We had a wonderful meeting. On the way there, the Lord showed me one woman who would be there. After I preached, I called her up. We anointed her and she fell out in the Spirit. She threw up on a napkin. She didn't testify to being healed yet. Offering was $29.

In October 1999, John Perry's church, Pentecostal Church of God. I preached on Mark 5. Hard to preach. Praise God. He is always there just in time.

On October 5, 1999, The Lord touched May Guthrie. She couldn't make her water pass. After prayer, she began to go to the bathroom. To God be the glory for everything. Praise God!

On November 4, 1999, I preached at John Perry's church. It was a Thursday night. I preached on Isaiah 53. There were 7 people there.

Thanksgiving, November 1999. John Perry's church. John 3:16. No one saved, but one prayed for. The Lord blessed. No offering.

September 2, 1999. John Perry's church. Pentecostal Holiness Church. I preached on John 3:16. There were 21 in attendance.

January 12, 2000. Robert's church at Walhalla. I preached about the lost coin, the lost sheep, and the prodigal son. Luke 15. The offering was $19. Several were prayed for. Praise God!

January 19, 2000. I preached at Brother Bryce's church in Pickens, SC. I preached on Luke 19. The issue of blood and Jairus' daughter.

February 17, 2000. John Perry's church. I preached on Jonah. 5 people present. 2 prayed for.

February 18, 2000. Pentecostal Holiness Church in Walhalla. Holy Ghost took over. Praise God!

March 2000. Eddie Middlin got saved. Me and Robert visited the hospital and a man got saved. Praise God!

April 5, 2000. At Robert's church, I was supposed to preach. I studied and studied, but God had not given me a message. When Robert got through singing, he started praying for the sick and he started praying for the sick. He started crying and preaching, so I knew God wanted him to preach. I said to let the Lord have his way. We sure did have a good service. Praise God!

April 2000. I preached at Brother Bryer's church. I preached on the crucifixion of Jesus. We had a good service and several got prayed for.

June 2, 2000. I preached at Brother Bryce's church. I preached on John 3:16 and several other chapters.

June 7, 2006. I shared my testimony about what God had done for me. Matthew 5. I preached on lit candles.

June 15, 2005. Me and Carol preached a revival at Dacusville Pentecostal Church of God. Matthew 5. I preached on lit candles. I got blessed. Offering was $39.

June 28, 2006. I preached in Woodruff. I preach on the Last Supper. The disciples followed Jesus to the Garden of Gethsemane. He told the disciples to watch and pray. Good revival. Offering was $46. God healed a woman.

January 2007. I preached at Joy Community Church of God. I preached on faith. The Lord blessed. No one got saved.

January 2007. Joy Community Church of God. I preached on love. The Lord blessed. No one saved.

Part Four

Healing Made Whole

CONCORDANCE OF SCRIPTURE
BY TOPIC

KING JAMES VERSION

Topic

HEALING

And Moses cried unto the Lᴏʀᴅ, saying, Heal her now, O God,
I beseech thee.

NUMBERS 12:13

See now that I, even I, am he, and there is no god with me: I kill, and I
make alive; I wound, and I heal: neither is there any that can deliver out of
my hand.

DEUTERONOMY 32:39

So the waters were healed unto this day, according to the saying of Elisha
which he spake.

2 KINGS 2:22

And Hezekiah said unto Isaiah, What shall be the sign that the Lᴏʀᴅ will heal
me, and that I shall go up into the house of the Lᴏʀᴅ the third day?

2 KINGS 20:8

And the Lᴏʀᴅ hearkened to Hezekiah, and healed the people.

2 CHRONICLES 30:20

Have mercy upon me, O Lᴏʀᴅ; for I am weak: O Lᴏʀᴅ, heal me; for my
bones are vexed.

PSALM 6:2

O Lᴏʀᴅ my God, I cried unto thee, and thou hast healed me.

PSALM 30:2

I said, Lᴏʀᴅ, be merciful unto me: heal my soul; for I have sinned
against thee.

PSALM 41:4

Who forgiveth all thine iniquities; who healeth all thy diseases;

PSALM 103:3

A time to kill, and a time to heal; a time to break down, and a time to build up;

ECCLESIASTES 3:3

But he was wounded for our transgressions, he was bruised for our iniquities: the chastisement of our peace was upon him; and with his stripes we are healed.

ISAIAH 53:5

Return, ye backsliding children, and I will heal your backslidings. Behold, we come unto thee; for thou art the LORD our God.

JEREMIAH 3:22

They have healed also the hurt of the daughter of my people slightly, saying, Peace, peace; when there is no peace.

JEREMIAH 4:14

Hast thou utterly rejected Judah? hath thy soul lothed Zion? why hast thou smitten us, and there is no healing for us? we looked for peace, and there is no good; and for the time of healing, and behold trouble!

JEREMIAH 14:19

Why is my pain perpetual, and my wound incurable, which refuseth to be healed? wilt thou be altogether unto me as a liar, and as waters that fail?

JEREMIAH 15:18

Heal me, O LORD, and I shall be healed; save me, and I shall be saved: for thou art my praise.

JEREMIAH 17:14

There is none to plead thy cause, that thou mayest be bound up: thou hast no healing medicines.

JEREMIAH 30:13

Then said he unto me, These waters issue out toward the east country, and go down into the desert, and go into the sea: which being brought forth into the sea, the waters shall be healed.

EZEKIEL 47:8

Come, and let us return unto the LORD: for he hath torn, and he will heal us; he hath smitten, and he will bind us up.

HOSEA 6:1

When I would have healed Israel, then the iniquity of Ephraim was discovered, and the wickedness of Samaria: for they commit falsehood; and the thief cometh in, and the troop of robbers spoileth without.

HOSEA 7:1

I will heal their backsliding, I will love them freely: for mine anger is turned away from him.

HOSEA 14:4

But unto you that fear my name shall the Sun of righteousness arise with healing in his wings; and ye shall go forth, and grow up as calves of the stall.

MALACHI 4:2

And Jesus went about all Galilee, teaching in their synagogues, and preaching the gospel of the kingdom, and healing all manner of sickness and all manner of disease among the people.

MATTHEW 4:23

And Jesus saith unto him, I will come and heal him.

MATTHEW 8:7

And Jesus went about all the cities and villages, teaching in their synagogues, and preaching the gospel of the kingdom, and healing every sickness and every disease among the people.

MATTHEW 9:35

And when he had called unto him his twelve disciples, he gave them power against unclean spirits, to cast them out, and to heal all manner of sickness and all manner of disease.

MATTHEW 10:1

And, behold, there was a man which had his hand withered. And they asked him, saying, Is it lawful to heal on the sabbath days? that they might accuse him.

MATTHEW 12:10

The Spirit of the Lord is upon me, because he hath anointed me to preach the gospel to the poor; he hath sent me to heal the brokenhearted, to preach deliverance to the captives, and recovering of sight to the blind, to set at liberty them that are bruised,

LUKE 4:18

And he said unto them, Ye will surely say unto me this proverb, Physician, heal thyself: whatsoever we have heard done in Capernaum, do also here in thy country.

LUKE 4:23

And it came to pass on a certain day, as he was teaching, that there were Pharisees and doctors of the law sitting by, which were come out of every town of Galilee, and Judaea, and Jerusalem: and the power of the Lord was present to heal them.

LUKE 5:17

And the whole multitude sought to touch him: for there went virtue out of him, and healed them all.

LUKE 6:19

And when he heard of Jesus, he sent unto him the elders of the Jews, beseeching him that he would come and heal his servant.

LUKE 7:3

And when the woman saw that she was not hid, she came trembling, and falling down before him, she declared unto him before all the people for what cause she had touched him, and how she was healed immediately.

LUKE 8:47

And they departed, and went through the towns, preaching the gospel, and healing every where.

LUKE 9:6

And Jesus answered and said, Suffer ye thus far. And he touched his ear, and healed him.

LUKE 22:51

When he heard that Jesus was come out of Judaea into Galilee, he went unto him, and besought him that he would come down, and heal his son: for he was at the point of death.

JOHN 4:47

And beholding the man which was healed standing with them, they could say nothing against it.

ACTS 4:14

For the man was above forty years old, on whom this miracle of healing was shewed.

ACTS 4:22

By stretching forth thine hand to heal; and that signs and wonders may be done by the name of thy holy child Jesus.

ACTS 4:30

There came also a multitude out of the cities round about unto Jerusalem, bringing sick folks, and them which were vexed with unclean spirits: and they were healed every one.

ACTS 5:16

How God anointed Jesus of Nazareth with the Holy Ghost and with power: who went about doing good, and healing all that were oppressed of the devil; for God was with him.

ACTS 10:38

The same heard Paul speak: who stedfastly beholding him, and perceiving that he had faith to be healed,
ACTS 14:9

To another faith by the same Spirit; to another the gifts of healing by the same Spirit;
1 CORINTHIANS 12:9

And make straight paths for your feet, lest that which is lame be turned out of the way; but let it rather be healed.
HEBREWS 12:13

Confess your faults one to another, and pray one for another, that ye may be healed. The effectual fervent prayer of a righteous man availeth much.
JAMES 5:16

Who his own self bare our sins in his own body on the tree, that we, being dead to sins, should live unto righteousness: by whose stripes ye were healed.
1 PETER 2:24

And I saw one of his heads as it were wounded to death; and his deadly wound was healed: and all the world wondered after the beast.
REVELATION 13:3

In the midst of the street of it, and on either side of the river, was there the tree of life, which bare twelve manner of fruits, and yielded her fruit every month: and the leaves of the tree were for the healing of the nations.
REVELATION 22:2

FAITH

RELIANCE

And he said, I will hide my face from them, I will see what their end shall be: for they are a very froward generation, children in whom is no faith.
DEUTERONOMY 32:20

Behold, his soul which is lifted up is not upright in him: but the just shall live by his faith.
HABAKKUK 2:4

Wherefore, if God so clothe the grass of the field, which to day is, and to morrow is cast into the oven, shall he not much more clothe you, O ye of little faith?
MATTHEW 6:30

When Jesus heard it, he marvelled, and said to them that followed, Verily I say unto you, I have not found so great faith, no, not in Israel.
MATTHEW 8:10

But Jesus turned him about, and when he saw her, he said, Daughter, be of good comfort; thy faith hath made thee whole. And the woman was made whole from that hour.
MATTHEW 9:22

Then touched he their eyes, saying, According to your faith be it unto you.
MATTHEW 9:29

And Jesus said unto them, Because of your unbelief: for verily I say unto you, If ye have faith as a grain of mustard seed, ye shall say unto this mountain, Remove hence to yonder place; and it shall remove; and nothing shall be impossible unto you.
MATTHEW 17:20

Jesus answered and said unto them, Verily I say unto you, If ye have faith, and doubt not, ye shall not only do this which is done to the fig tree, but also if ye shall say unto this mountain, Be thou removed, and be thou cast into the sea; it shall be done.

MATTHEW 21:21

Woe unto you, scribes and Pharisees, hypocrites! for ye pay tithe of mint and anise and cummin, and have omitted the weightier matters of the law, judgment, mercy, and faith: these ought ye to have done, and not to leave the other undone.

MATTHEW 23:23

And he said unto them, Why are ye so fearful? how is it that ye have no faith?

MARK 4:40

And Jesus answering saith unto them, Have faith in God.

MARK 11:22

And he said to the woman, Thy faith hath saved thee; go in peace.

LUKE 7:50

And the apostles said unto the Lord, Increase our faith.

LUKE 17:5

I tell you that he will avenge them speedily. Nevertheless when the Son of man cometh, shall he find faith on the earth?

LUKE 18:8

But I have prayed for thee, that thy faith fail not: and when thou art converted, strengthen thy brethern.

LUKE 22:32

And he came out, and went, as he was wont, to the mount of Olives; and his disciples also followed him.

LUKE 22:39

And his name through faith in his name hath made this man strong, whom ye see and know: yea, the faith which is by him hath given him this perfect soundness in the presence of you all.

ACTS 3:16

For Moses truly said unto the fathers, A prophet shall the Lord your God raise up unto you of your brethren, like unto me; him shall ye hear in all things whatsoever he shall say unto you.

ACTS 3:22

And when they were come, and had gathered the church together, they rehearsed all that God had done with them, and how he had opened the door of faith unto the Gentiles.

ACTS 14:27

And put no difference between us and them, purifying their hearts by faith.

ACTS 15:9

And so were the churches established in the faith, and increased in number daily.

ACTS 16:5

Testifying both to the Jews, and also to the Greeks, repentance toward God, and faith toward our Lord Jesus Christ.

ACTS 20:21

And after certain days, when Felix came with his wife Drusilla, which was a Jewess, he sent for Paul, and heard him concerning the faith in Christ.

ACTS 24:24

To open their eyes, and to turn them from darkness to light, and from the power of Satan unto God, that they may receive forgiveness of sins, and inheritance among them which are sanctified by faith that is in me.

ACTS 26:18

By whom we have received grace and apostleship, for obedience to the faith among all nations, for his name:

ROMANS 1:5

For therein is the righteousness of God revealed from faith to faith: as it is written, The just shall live by faith.

ROMANS 1:17

For what if some did not believe? shall their unbelief make the faith of God without effect?

ROMANS 3:3

Whom God hath set forth to be a propitiation through faith in his blood, to declare his righteousness for the remission of sins that are past, through the forbearance of God;

ROMANS 3:25

But to him that worketh not, but believeth on him that justifieth the ungodly, his faith is counted for righteousness.

ROMANS 4:5

For the promise, that he should be the heir of the world, was not to Abraham, or to his seed, through the law, but through the righteousness of faith.

ROMANS 4:13

Therefore it is of faith, that it might be by grace; to the end the promise might be sure to all the seed; not to that only which is of the law, but to that also which is of the faith of Abraham; who is the father of us all,

ROMANS 4:16

And being not weak in faith, he considered not his own body now dead, when he was about an hundred years old, neither yet the deadness of Sarah's womb: He staggered not at the promise of God through unbelief; but was strong in faith, giving glory to God;

ROMANS 4:19,20

Therefore being justified by faith, we have peace with God through our Lord Jesus Christ: By whom also we have access by faith into this grace wherein we stand, and rejoice in hope of the glory of God.

ROMANS 5:1,2

By whom also we have access by faith into this grace wherein we stand, and rejoice in hope of the glory of God.

ROMANS 10:8

For I say, through the grace given unto me, to every man that is among you, not to think of himself more highly than he ought to think; but to think soberly, according as God hath dealt to every man the measure of faith.

ROMANS 12:3

Having then gifts differing according to the grace that is given to us, whether prophecy, let us prophesy according to the proportion of faith;

ROMANS 12:6

Him that is weak in the faith receive ye, but not to doubtful disputations.

ROMANS 14:1

Hast thou faith? have it to thyself before God. Happy is he that condemneth not himself in that thing which he alloweth. And he that doubteth is damned if he eat, because he eateth not of faith: for whatsoever is not of faith is sin.

ROMANS 14:22,23

That your faith should not stand in the wisdom of men, but in the power of God.

1 CORINTHIANS 2:5

Now we have received, not the spirit of the world, but the spirit which is of God; that we might know the things that are freely given to us of God.

1 CORINTHIANS 2:12

To another faith by the same Spirit; to another the gifts of healing by the same Spirit;

1 CORINTHIANS 12:9

And though I have the gift of prophecy, and understand all mysteries, and all knowledge; and though I have all faith, so that I could remove mountains, and have not charity, I am nothing.

1 CORINTHIANS 13:2

And now abideth faith, hope, charity, these three; but the greatest of these is charity.

1 CORINTHIANS 13:13

And if Christ be not risen, then is our preaching vain, and your faith is also vain.

1 CORINTHIANS 15:14

Watch ye, stand fast in the faith, quit you like men, be strong.

1 CORINTHIANS 16:13

Not for that we have dominion over your faith, but are helpers of your joy: for by faith ye stand.

2 CORINTHIANS 1:24

We having the same spirit of faith, according as it is written, I believed, and therefore have I spoken; we also believe, and therefore speak;

2 CORINTHIANS 4:13

(For we walk by faith, not by sight:)

2 CORINTHIANS 5:7

Examine yourselves, whether ye be in the faith; prove your own selves. Know ye not your own selves, how that Jesus Christ is in you, except ye be reprobates?

2 CORINTHIANS 13:5

But they had heard only, That he which persecuted us in times past now preacheth the faith which once he destroyed.

GALATIANS 1:23

I am crucified with Christ: nevertheless I live; yet not I, but Christ liveth in me: and the life which I now live in the flesh I live by the faith of the Son of God, who loved me, and gave himself for me.

GALATIANS 2:20

This only would I learn of you, Received ye the Spirit by the works of the law, or by the hearing of faith?

GALATIANS 3:2

But the scripture hath concluded all under sin, that the promise by faith of Jesus Christ might be given to them that believe.

GALATIANS 3:22

For in Jesus Christ niether circumcision availeth any thing, nor uncircumcision; but faith which worketh by love.

GALATIANS 5:6

But the fruit of the Spirit is love, joy, peace, longsuffering, gentleness, goodness, faith, Meekness, temperance: against such there is no law.

GALATIANS 5:22,23

As we have therefore opportunity, let us do good unto all men, especially unto them who are of the household of faith.

GALATIANS 6:10

One Lord, one faith, one baptism,

EPHESIANS 4:5

Till we all come in the unity of the faith, and of the knowledge of the Son of God, unto a perfect man, unto the measure of the stature of the fulness of Christ:

EPHESIANS 4:13

Above all, taking the shield of faith, wherewith ye shall be able to quench all the fiery darts of the wicked.

EPHESIANS 6:16

Peace be to the brethren, and love with faith, from God the Father and the Lord Jesus Christ.

EPHESIANS 6:23

And having this confidence, I know that I shall abide and continue with you all for your furtherance and joy of faith;

PHILIPPIANS 1:25

Only let your conversation be as it becometh the gospel of Christ: that whether I come and see you, or else be absent, I may hear of your affairs, that ye stand fast in one spirit, with one mind striving together for the faith of the gospel;

PHILIPPIANS 1:27

If ye continue in the faith grounded and settled, and be not moved away from the hope of the gospel, which ye have heard, and which was preached to every creature which is under heaven; whereof I Paul am made a minister;

COLOSSIANS 1:23

For though I be absent in the flesh, yet am I with you in the spirit, joying and beholding your order, and the stedfastness of your faith in Christ.

COLOSSIANS 2:5

Remembering without ceasing your work of faith, and labour of love, and patience of hope in our Lord Jesus Christ, in the sight of God and our Father;

1 THESSALONIANS 1:3

But let us, who are of the day, be sober, putting on the breastplate of faith and love; and for an helmet, the hope of salvation.

1 THESSALONIANS 5:8

We are bound to thank God always for you, brethren, as it is meet, because that your faith groweth exceedingly, and the charity of every one of you all toward each other aboundeth; So that we ourselves glory in you in the churches of God for your patience and faith in all your persecutions and tribulations that ye endure:

2 THESSALONIANS 1:3,4

And that we may be delivered from unreasonable and wicked men: for all men have not faith.

2 THESSALONIANS 3:2

Unto Timothy, my own son in the faith: Grace, mercy, and peace, from God our Father and Jesus Christ our Lord.

1 TIMOTHY 1:2

Now the end of the commandment is charity out of a pure heart, and of a good conscience, and of faith unfeigned:

1 TIMOTHY 1:5

Holding faith, and a good conscience; which some having put away concerning faith have made shipwreck:

1 TIMOTHY 1:19

Notwithstanding she shall be saved in childbearing, if they continue in faith and charity and holiness with sobriety.

1 TIMOTHY 2:15

Holding the mystery of the faith in a pure conscience.

1 TIMOTHY 3:9

For they that have used the office of a deacon well purchase to themselves a good degree, and great boldness in the faith which is in Christ Jesus.

1 TIMOTHY 3:13

Now the Spirit speaketh expressly, that in the latter times some shall depart from the faith, giving heed to seducing spirits, and doctrines of devils;

1 TIMOTHY 4:1

But if any provide not for his own, and specially for those of his own house, he hath denied the faith, and is worse than an infidel.

1 TIMOTHY 5:8

For the love of money is the root of all evil: which while some coveted after, they have erred from the faith, and pierced themselves through with many sorrows.

1 TIMOTHY 6:10

Fight the good fight of faith, lay hold on eternal life, whereunto thou art also called, and hast professed a good profession before many witnesses.

1 TIMOTHY 6:12

When I call to remembrance the unfeigned faith that is in thee, which dwelt first in thy grandmother Lois, and thy mother Eunice; and I am persuaded that in thee also.

2 TIMOTHY 1:5

Who concerning the truth have erred, saying that the resurrection is past already; and overthrow the faith of some.

2 TIMOTHY 2:18

Now as Jannes and Jambres withstood Moses, so do these also resist the truth: men of corrupt minds, reprobate concerning the faith.

2 TIMOTHY 3:8

I have fought a good fight, I have finished my course, I have kept the faith:

2 TIMOTHY 4:7

Paul, a servant of God, and an apostle of Jesus Christ, according to the faith of God's elect, and the acknowledging of the truth which is after godliness;

TITUS 1:1

This witness is true. Wherefore rebuke them sharply, that they may be sound in the faith;

TITUS 1:13

For unto us was the gospel preached, as well as unto them: but the word preached did not profit them, not being mixed with faith in them that heard it.

HEBREWS 4:2

Therefore leaving the principles of the doctrine of Christ, let us go on unto perfection; not laying again the foundation of repentance from dead works, and of faith toward God,

HEBREWS 6:1

That ye be not slothful, but followers of them who through faith and patience inherit the promises.

HEBREWS 6:12

Let us draw near with a true heart in full assurance of faith, having our hearts sprinkled from an evil conscience, and our bodies washed with pure water.

HEBREWS 10:22

Now faith is the substance of things hoped for, the evidence of things not seen.

HEBREWS 11:1

But without faith it is impossible to please him: for he that cometh to God must believe that he is, and that he is a rewarder of them that diligently seek him.

HEBREWS 11:6

And these all, having obtained a good report through faith, received not the promise:

HEBREWS 11:39

Looking unto Jesus the author and finisher of our faith; who for the joy that was set before him endured the cross, despising the shame, and is set down at the right hand of the throne of God.

HEBREWS 12:2

Remember them which have the rule over you, who have spoken unto you the word of God: whose faith follow, considering the end of their conversation.

HEBREWS 13:7

Knowing this, that the trying of your faith worketh patience.

JAMES 1:3

But let him ask in faith, nothing wavering. For he that wavereth is like a wave of the sea driven with the wind and tossed.

JAMES 1:6

My brethren, have not the faith of our Lord Jesus Christ, the Lord of glory, with respect of persons.

JAMES 2:1

Hearken, my beloved brethren, Hath not God chosen the poor of this world rich in faith, and heirs of the kingdom which he hath promised to them that love him?

JAMES 2:5

What doth it profit, my brethren, though a man say he hath faith, and have not works? can faith save him? Hearken, my beloved brethern, Hath not God chosen the poor of this world rich in faith, and heirs of the kingdom which he hath promised to them that love him?

JAMES 2:14,15

Even so faith, if it hath not works, is dead, being alone. Yea, a man may say, Thou hast faith, and I have works: shew me thy faith without thy works, and I will shew thee my faith by my works.

JAMES 2:17,18

But wilt thou know, O vain man, that faith without works is dead?

JAMES 2:20

Seest thou how faith wrought with his works, and by works was faith made perfect?

JAMES 2:22

And the prayer of faith shall save the sick, and the Lord shall raise him up; and if he have committed sins, they shall be forgiven him.

JAMES 5:15

Receiving the end of your faith, even the salvation of your souls.

1 PETER 1:9

Whom resist stedfast in the faith, knowing that the same afflictions are accomplished in your brethren that are in the world.

1 PETER 5:9

Simon Peter, a servant and an apostle of Jesus Christ, to them that have obtained like precious faith with us through the righteousness of God and our Saviour Jesus Christ:

2 PETER 1:1

And beside this, giving all diligence, add to your faith virtue; and to virtue knowledge;

2 PETER 1:5

For whatsoever is born of God overcometh the world: and this is the victory that overcometh the world, even our faith.

1 JOHN 5:4

Beloved, when I gave all diligence to write unto you of the common salvation, it was needful for me to write unto you, and exhort you that ye should earnestly contend for the faith which was once delivered unto the saints.

JUDE 1:3

But ye, beloved, building up yourselves on your most holy faith, praying in the Holy Ghost,

JUDE 1:20

I know thy works, and where thou dwellest, even where Satan's seat is: and thou holdest fast my name, and hast not denied my faith, even in those days wherein Antipas was my faithful martyr, who was slain among you, where Satan dwelleth.

REVELATION 2:13

Because thou hast kept the word of my patience, I also will keep thee from the hour of temptation, which shall come upon all the world, to try them that dwell upon the earth.

REVELATION 3:10

He that leadeth into captivity shall go into captivity: he that killeth with the sword must be killed with the sword. Here is the patience and the faith of the saints.

REVELATION 13:10

Here is the patience of the saints: here are they that keep the commandments of God, and the faith of Jesus.

REVELATION 14:12

CHARITY

Now as touching things offered unto idols, we know that we all have knowledge. Knowledge puffeth up, but charity edifieth.

1 CORINTHIANS 8:1

Though I speak with the tongues of men and of angels, and have not charity, I am become as sounding brass, or a tinkling cymbal. And though I have the gift of prophecy, and understand all mysteries, and all knowledge; and though I have all faith, so that I could remove mountains, and have not charity, I am nothing.

1 CORINTHIANS 13:1,2

Charity suffereth long, and is kind; charity envieth not; charity vaunteth not itself, is not puffed up,

1 CORINTHIANS 13:4

Charity never faileth: but whether there be prophecies, they shall fail; whether there be tongues, they shall cease; whether there be knowledge, it shall vanish away.

1 CORINTHIANS 13:8

And now abideth faith, hope, charity, these three; but the greatest of these is charity.

1 CORINTHIANS 13:13

Follow after charity, and desire spiritual gifts, but rather that ye may prophesy.

1 CORINTHIANS 14:1

Let all your things be done with charity.

1 CORINTHIANS 16:14

And above all these things put on charity, which is the bond of perfectness.

COLOSSIANS 3:14

But now when Timotheus came from you unto us, and brought us good tidings of your faith and charity, and that ye have good remembrance of us always, desiring greatly to see us, as we also to see you:

1 THESSALONIANS 3:6

We are bound to thank God always for you, brethren, as it is meet, because that your faith groweth exceedingly, and the charity of every one of you all toward each other aboundeth;

2 THESSALONIANS 1:3

Now the end of the commandment is charity out of a pure heart, and of a good conscience, and of faith unfeigned:

1 TIMOTHY 1:5

Notwithstanding she shall be saved in childbearing, if they continue in faith and charity and holiness with sobriety.

1 TIMOTHY 2:15

Let no man despise thy youth; but be thou an example of the believers, in word, in conversation, in charity, in spirit, in faith, in purity.

1 TIMOTHY 4:12

Flee also youthful lusts: but follow righteousness, faith, charity, peace, with them that call on the Lord out of a pure heart.

2 TIMOTHY 2:22

But thou hast fully known my doctrine, manner of life, purpose, faith, longsuffering, charity, patience,

2 TIMOTHY 3:10

That the aged men be sober, grave, temperate, sound in faith, in charity, in patience.

TITUS 2:2

And above all things have fervent charity among yourselves: for charity shall cover the multitude of sins.

1 PETER 4:8

Greet ye one another with a kiss of charity. Peace be with you all that are in Christ Jesus. Amen.

1 PETER 5:14

And to godliness brotherly kindness; and to brotherly kindness charity.

2 PETER 1:7

Which have borne witness of thy charity before the church: whom if thou bring forward on their journey after a godly sort, thou shalt do well:

3 JOHN 1:6

I know thy works, and charity, and service, and faith, and thy patience, and thy works; and the last to be more than the first.

REVELATION 2:19

UNITY

UNITY MEANS ONENESS, SINGLENESS.

UNITY OF BELIEVERS

So we, being many, are one body in Christ, and every one members one of another.

ROMANS 12:5

For we being many are one bread, and one body: for we are all partakers of that one bread.

1 CORINTHIANS 10:17

There is neither Jew nor Greek, there is neither bond nor free, there is neither male nor female: for ye are all one in Christ Jesus.

GALATIANS 3:28

UNITY OF THE FAITH

Faith is what moves mountains. Unity is what moves disharmony and discord and replaces it with love and kindness.

Endeavouring to keep the unity of the Spirit in the bond of peace.

EPHESIANS 4:3

The Holy Ghost works in a Spirit of Unity that fell upon the early church because it had unity.

There is one body, and one Spirit, even as ye are called in one hope of your calling;

EPHESIANS 4:4

Till we all come in the unity of the faith, and of the knowledge of the Son of God, unto a perfect man, unto the measure of the stature of the fulness of Christ:

EPHESIANS 4:13

True unity is not man-made. It is the Spirit of God that runs through us that brings us together as oneness.

Only let your conversation be as it becometh the gospel of Christ: that whether I come and see you, or else be absent, I may hear of your affairs, that ye stand fast in one spirit, with one mind striving together for the faith of the gospel;

PHILIPPIANS 1:27

Unity is like a flood. It covers all the land. And the land that divides become as one in water. Like we all become one in the Spirit.

Unity of the Spirit is like oceans of love.

UNITY OF THE FAITH

The Church has a purpose in the world. It is not of the world, but in the world. The early church had one thing in common. They were all united. They would pray together. The Church would come together in unity to worship the Lord and have fellowship. God unified all the church bodies to make them into one body. And their purpose was to win the lost. That their lives would change forever. They would become part of the unity of Christ. Jesus Christ will win the world. Jesus prayed for unity in the Gospel of John.

That they all may be one; as thou, Father, art in me, and I in thee, that they also may be one in us: that the world may believe that thou hast sent me.

JOHN 17:21

Behold, how good and how pleasant it is for brethren to dwell together in unity!

PSALM 133:1

JESUS HEALS THE SICK

And said, If thou wilt diligently hearken to the voice of the Lord thy God, and wilt do that which is right in his sight, and wilt give ear to his commandments, and keep all his statutes, I will put none of these diseases upon thee, which I have brought upon the Egyptians: for I am the Lord that healeth thee.

EXODUS 15:26

The Lord Jesus Christ is still the healer. He cannot change: for Jesus Christ is the same yesterday and today, and forever! He is still with us today! For He said, I am with you all the days, even unto the consummation of the ages!

And the men of the city said unto Elisha, Behold, I pray thee, the situation of this city is pleasant, as my lord seeth: but the water is naught, and the ground barren.

2 KINGS 2:19

So the waters were healed unto this day, according to the saying of Elisha which he spake.

2 KINGS 2:22

God's way of healing a person is not a thing Jesus said. This is what he said: I am the way, and the truth, and the life, and He has ever been reliable to His people in all the ages. By the covenant name, Jehovah Rophi: I am Jehovah that (healeth) thee!

Then she came and told the man of God. And he said, Go, sell the oil, and pay thy debt, and live thou and thy children of the rest.

2 KINGS 4:7

And when Elisha was come into the house, behold, the child was dead, and laid upon his bed. He went in therefore, and shut the door upon them twain, and prayed unto the LORD.

2 KINGS 4:32,33

Then he returned, and walked in the house to and fro; and went up, and stretched himself upon him: and the child sneezed seven times, and the child opened his eyes.

2 KINGS 4:35

So Naaman came with his horses and with his chariot, and stood at the door of the house of Elisha. And Elisha sent a messenger unto him, saying, Go and wash in Jordan seven times, and thy flesh shall come again to thee, and thou shalt be clean.

2 KINGS 5:9,10

Then went he down, and dipped himself seven times in Jordan, according to the saying of the man of God: and his flesh came again like unto the flesh of a little child, and he was clean.

2 KINGS 5:14

Surely he hath borne our griefs, and carried our sorrows: yet we did esteem him stricken, smitten of God, and afflicted. But he was wounded for our transgressions, he was bruised for our iniquities: the chastisement of our peace was upon him; and with his stripes we are healed.

ISAIAH 53:4,5

That it might be fulfilled which was spoken by Esaias the prophet, saying, Himself took our infirmities, and bare our sicknesses.

MATTHEW 8:17

Diseases are the devil's works. Consequences of sin. And it is impossible for the will of the devil to be the will of God. Christ came to destroy the works of the devil. And when Christ walked upon the earth, He healed all manner of diseases and sicknesses. Jesus went about doing good and healing all that were oppressed of the devil.

While he spake these things unto them, behold, there came a certain ruler, and worshipped him, saying, My daughter is even now dead: but come and lay thy hand upon her, and she shall live.

MATTHEW 9:18

But when the people were put forth, he went in, and took her by the hand, and the maid arose.

MATTHEW 9:25

Then Jesus answered and said unto her, O woman, great is thy faith: be it unto thee even as thou wilt. And her daughter was made whole from that very hour.

MATTHEW 15:28

They say unto him, Lord, that our eyes may be opened. So Jesus had compassion on them, and touched their eyes: and immediately their eyes received sight, and they followed him.

MATTHEW 20:33,34

Teaching them to observe all things whatsoever I have commanded you: and, lo, I am with you always, even unto the end of the world. Amen.

MATTHEW 28:20

Because He is unchangeable and, because He is the healer of His people. It was prophesied of Him. Surely He hath borne our griefs. And with His stripes, we are healed, and it is expressed and also declared that this was fulfilled in His ministry of healing which still continues today. This is found in Isaiah 53:4,5 and Matthew 8:17.

Mark 1:23 - And there was in their synagogue a man with an unclean spirit; and he cried out,

MARK 1:23

And Jesus rebuked him, saying, Hold thy peace, and come out of him. And when the unclean spirit had torn him, and cried with a loud voice, he came out of him.

MARK 1:25,26

But Simon's wife's mother lay sick of a fever, and anon they tell him of her. And he came and took her by the hand, and lifted her up; and immediately the fever left her, and she ministered unto them.

MARK 1:30,31

And there came a leper to him, beseeching him, and kneeling down to him, and saying unto him, If thou wilt, thou canst make me clean.

MARK 1:40

And they come unto him, bringing one sick of the palsy, which was borne of four.

MARK 2:3

But that ye may know that the Son of man hath power on earth to forgive sins, (he saith to the sick of the palsy,) I say unto thee, Arise, and take up thy bed, and go thy way into thine house.

MARK 2:10,11

And they watched him, whether he would heal him on the sabbath day; that they might accuse him.

MARK 3:2

This man had a withered hand!

And when he had looked round about on them with anger, being grieved for the hardness of their hearts, he saith unto the man, Stretch forth thine hand. And he stretched it out: and his hand was restored whole as the other.

MARK 3:5

This is a time that Jesus cast out devils that tormented a man for years. Jesus saw a head of swine and cast the devils into them.

And straightway his ears were opened, and the string of his tongue was loosed, and he spake plain.

MARK 3:35

And Jesus went about all Galilee, teaching in their synagogues, and preaching the gospel of the kingdom, and healing all manner of sickness and all manner of disease among the people.

MATTHEW 4:23

And he took the damsel by the hand, and said unto her, Talitha cumi; which is, being interpreted, Damsel, I say unto thee, arise. And straightway the damsel arose, and walked; for she was of the age of twelve years. And they were astonished with a great astonishment.

MARK 5:41,42

Still today, people are astonished when the power of God moves in a mighty way of healing. His power is awesome. He also heals people of unclean spirits just like thousands of years ago. He still does it today. And His power is still awesome!

And he said unto her, For this saying go thy way; the devil is gone out of thy daughter.

MARK 7:29

And they bring unto him one that was deaf, and had an impediment in his speech; and they beseech him to put his hand upon him. And he took him aside from the multitude, and put his fingers into his ears, and he spit, and touched his tongue;

MARK 7:32,33

And he cometh to Bethsaida; and they bring a blind man unto him, and besought him to touch him.

MARK 8:22

After that he put his hands again upon his eyes, and made him look up: and he was restored, and saw every man clearly.

MARK 8:25

And one of the multitude answered and said, Master, I have brought unto thee my son, which hath a dumb spirit;

MARK 9:17

When Jesus saw that the people came running together, he rebuked the foul spirit, saying unto him, Thou dumb and deaf spirit, I charge thee, come out of him, and enter no more into him.

MARK 9:25

And they came to Jericho: and as he went out of Jericho with his disciples and a great number of people, blind Bartimaeus, the son of Timaeus, sat by the highway side begging.

MARK 10:46

And it came to pass, when he was in a certain city, behold a man full of leprosy: who seeing Jesus fell on his face, and besought him, saying, Lord, if thou wilt, thou canst make me clean. And he put forth his hand, and touched him, saying, I will: be thou clean. And immediately the leprosy departed from him.

LUKE 5:12,13

And it came to pass on a certain day, as he was teaching, that there were Pharisees and doctors of the law sitting by, which were come out of every town of Galilee, and Judaea, and Jerusalem: and the power of the Lord was present to heal them. And, behold, men brought in a bed a man which was taken with a palsy: and they sought means to bring him in, and to lay him before him. And when they could not find by what way they might bring him in because of the multitude, they went upon the housetop, and let him down through the tiling with his couch into the midst before Jesus. And when he saw their faith, he said unto him, Man, thy sins are forgiven thee.

LUKE 5:17-20

And the man with palsy was healed completely!

And a certain centurion's servant, who was dear unto him, was sick, and ready to die.

LUKE 7:2

And they that were sent, returning to the house, found the servant whole that had been sick.

LUKE 7:10

And when he went forth to land, there met him out of the city a certain man, which had devils long time, and ware no clothes, neither abode in any house, but in the tombs.

LUKE 8:27

Then went the devils out of the man, and entered into the swine: and the herd ran violently down a steep place into the lake, and were choked.

LUKE 8:33

They also which saw it told them by what means he that was possessed of the devils was healed.

LUKE 8:36

And a woman having an issue of blood twelve years, which had spent all her living upon physicians, neither could be healed of any,

LUKE 8:43

And when the woman saw that she was not hid, she came trembling, and falling down before him, she declared unto him before all the people for what cause she had touched him, and how she was healed immediately.

LUKE 8:47

To understand these verses, to understand the fullness, read each chapter of each verse that I have given throughout this book. These are some awesome healings that the Bible tells us about, but the healings don't stop here. There are healings happening here and around the world today. The Bible tells us that these things come by fasting and praying.

And, behold, a man of the company cried out, saying, Master, I beseech thee, look upon my son: for he is mine only child.

LUKE 9:38

And as he was yet a coming, the devil threw him down, and tare him. And Jesus rebuked the unclean spirit, and healed the child, and delivered him again to his father.

LUKE 9:42

And, behold, there was a woman which had a spirit of infirmity eighteen years, and was bowed together, and could in no wise lift up herself. And when Jesus saw her, he called her to him, and said unto her, Woman, thou art loosed from thine infirmity.

LUKE 13:11,12

And when he had said these things, all his adversaries were ashamed: and all the people rejoiced for all the glorious things that were done by him.

LUKE 13:17

And as he entered into a certain village, there met him ten men that were lepers, which stood afar off: And they lifted up their voices, and said, Jesus, Master, have mercy on us. And when he saw them, he said unto them, Go shew yourselves unto the priests. And it came to pass, that, as they went, they were cleansed.

LUKE 17:12-14

And it came to pass, that as he was come nigh unto Jericho, a certain blind man sat by the way side begging:

LUKE 18:35

And immediately he received his sight, and followed him, glorifying God: and all the people, when they saw it, gave praise unto God.

LUKE 18:43

The impotent man answered him, Sir, I have no man, when the water is troubled, to put me into the pool: but while I am coming, another steppeth down before me. Jesus saith unto him, Rise, take up thy bed, and walk. And Immediately the man was made whole, and took up his bed, and walked: and on the same day was the sabbath.

JOHN 5:7-9

Then said Thomas, which is called Didymus, unto his fellow disciples, Let us also go, that we may die with him.

JOHN 11:16

And when he thus had spoken, he cried with a loud voice, Lazarus, come forth. And he that was dead came forth, bound hand and foot with graveclothes: and his face was bound about with a napkin. Jesus saith unto them, Loose him, and let him go.

JOHN 11:43,44

Jesus saith unto him, I am the way, the truth, and the life: no man cometh unto the Father, but by me.

JOHN 14:6

Insomuch that they brought forth the sick into the streets, and laid them on beds and couches, that at the least the shadow of Peter passing by might overshadow some of them. There came also a multitude out of the cities round about unto Jerusalem, bringing sick folks, and them which were vexed with unclean spirits: and they were healed every one.

ACTS 5:15,16

And it came to pass, as Peter passed throughout all quarters, he came down also to the saints which dwelt at Lydda. And there he found a certain man named Aeneas, which had kept his bed eight years, and was sick of the palsy. And Peter said unto him, Aeneas, Jesus Christ maketh thee whole: arise, and make thy bed. And he arose immediately. And all that dwelt at Lydda and Saron saw him, and turned to the Lord. Now there was at Joppa a certain disciple named Tabitha, which by interpretation is called Dorcas: this woman was full of good works and almsdeeds which she did. And it came to pass in those days, that she was sick, and died: whom when they had washed, they laid her in an upper chamber. And forasmuch as Lydda was nigh to Joppa, and the disciples had heard that Peter was there, they sent unto him two men, desiring him that he would not delay to come to them. Then Peter arose and went with them. When he was come, they brought him into the upper chamber: and all the widows stood by him weeping, and shewing the coats and garments which Dorcas made, while she was with them. But Peter put them all forth, and kneeled down, and prayed; and turning him to the body said, Tabitha, arise. And she opened her eyes: and when she saw Peter, she sat up. And he gave her his hand, and lifted her up, and when he had called the saints and widows, presented her alive. And it was known throughout all Joppa; and many believed in the Lord. And it came to pass, that he tarried many days in Joppa with one Simon a tanner.

ACTS 9:32-43

How God anointed Jesus of Nazareth with the Holy Ghost and with power: who went about doing good, and healing all that were oppressed of the devil; for God was with him.

ACTS 10:38

And it came to pass, that the father of Publius lay sick of a fever and of a bloody flux: to whom Paul entered in, and prayed, and laid his hands on him, and healed him. So when this was done, others also, which had diseases in the island, came, and were healed:

ACTS 28:8,9

Jesus Christ the same yesterday, and to day, and for ever.

HEBREWS 13:8

He that committeth sin is of the devil; for the devil sinneth from the beginning. For this purpose the Son of God was manifested, that he might destroy the works of the devil.

1 JOHN 3:8

THE GIFT OF HEALING

Here are the four prayers to the gift of healing:

The first is the direct prayer of faith. The second is intercessory prayer of two or more people. The third is the anointing of the elders of the church. And the fourth, the laying on of hands of those who believe and whom God had prepared and called to that ministry.

Thus saith thy Lord the LORD, and thy God that pleadeth the cause of his people, Behold, I have taken out of thine hand the cup of trembling, even the dregs of the cup of my fury; thou shalt no more drink it again: But I will put it into the hand of them that afflict thee; which have said to thy soul, Bow down, that we may go over: and thou hast laid thy body as the ground, and as the street, to them that went over.

ISAIAH 51:22,23

And when Jesus was entered into Capernaum, there came unto him a centurion, beseeching him,

MATTHEW 8:5

And Jesus said unto the centurion, Go thy way; and as thou hast believed, so be it done unto thee. And his servant was healed in the selfsame hour.

MATTHEW 8:13

Again I say unto you, That if two of you shall agree on earth as touching any thing that they shall ask, it shall be done for them of my Father which is in heaven.

MATTHEW 18:19

They shall take up serpents; and if they drink any deadly thing, it shall not hurt them; they shall lay hands on the sick, and they shall recover.

MARK 16:18

Divine Healing is oppressed by diabolical counterfeits. Among those are Christian Science, falsely so called mind healing. Spiritualism, trace evangelism, etc...

Now the Spirit speaketh expressly, that in the latter times some shall depart from the faith, giving heed to seducing spirits, and doctrines of devils; Speaking lies in hypocrisy; having their conscience seared with a hot iron;

1 TIMOTHY 4:1,2

O Timothy, keep that which is committed to thy trust, avoiding profane and vain babblings, and oppositions of science falsely so called: Which some professing have erred concerning the faith. Grace be with thee. Amen.

1 TIMOTHY 6:20,21

Is any sick among you? let him call for the elders of the church; and let them pray over him, anointing him with oil in the name of the Lord: And the prayer of faith shall save the sick, and the Lord shall raise him up; and if he have committed sins, they shall be forgiven him.

JAMES 5:14,15

Faith comes by hearing and the hearing by the Word of God. Jesus heals people!

HOPE

HOPE IN LOVE

CONFIDENT EXPECTATION

Turn again, my daughters, go your way; for I am too old to have an husband. If I should say, I have hope, if I should have an husband also to night, and should also bear sons;

RUTH 1:12

So the poor hath hope, and iniquity stoppeth her mouth.

JOB 5:16

My days are swifter than a weaver's shuttle, and are spent without hope.

JOB 7:6

So are the paths of all that forget God; and the hypocrite's hope shall perish: Whose hope shall be cut off, and whose trust shall be a spider's web.

JOB 8:13,14

For there is hope of a tree, if it be cut down, that it will sprout again, and that the tender branch thereof will not cease.

JOB 14:7

And where is now my hope? as for my hope, who shall see it?

JOB 17:15

He hath destroyed me on every side, and I am gone: and mine hope hath he removed like a tree.

JOB 19:10

For what is the hope of the hypocrite, though he hath gained, when God taketh away his soul?

JOB 27:8

Therefore my heart is glad, and my glory rejoiceth: my flesh also shall rest in hope.

PSALM 16:9

And now, Lord, what wait I for? my hope is in thee.

PSALM 39:7

That they might set their hope in God, and not forget the works of God, but keep his commandments:

PSALM 78:7

Uphold me according unto thy word, that I may live: and let me not be ashamed of my hope.

PSALM 119:116

Happy is he that hath the God of Jacob for his help, whose hope is in the LORD his God:

PSALM 146:5

Hope deferred maketh the heart sick: but when the desire cometh, it is a tree of life.

PROVERBS 13:12

The wicked is driven away in his wickedness: but the righteous hath hope in his death.

PROVERBS 14:32

Chasten thy son while there is hope, and let not thy soul spare for his crying.

PROVERBS 19:18

Seest thou a man wise in his own conceit? there is more hope of a fool than of him.

PROVERBS 26:12

For to him that is joined to all the living there is hope: for a living dog is better than a dead lion.

O the hope of Israel, the saviour thereof in time of trouble, why shouldest thou be as a stranger in the land, and as a wayfaring man that turneth aside to tarry for a night?

JEREMIAH 14:8

Blessed is the man that trusteth in the LORD, and whose hope the LORD is.

JEREMIAH 17:7

And there is hope in thine end, saith the LORD, that thy children shall come again to their own border.

JEREMIAH 31:7

Then he said unto me, Son of man, these bones are the whole house of Israel: behold, they say, Our bones are dried, and our hope is lost: we are cut off for our parts.

EZEKIEL 37:11

And I will give her her vineyards from thence, and the valley of Achor for a door of hope: and she shall sing there, as in the days of her youth, and as in the day when she came up out of the land of Egypt.

HOSEA 2:15

Turn you to the strong hold, ye prisoners of hope: even to day do I declare that I will render double unto thee;

ZECHARIAH 9:12

And when her masters saw that the hope of their gains was gone, they caught Paul and Silas, and drew them into the marketplace unto the rulers,

ACTS 16:19

And now I stand and am judged for the hope of the promise made of God, unto our fathers:

ACTS 26:6

And when neither sun nor stars in many days appeared, and no small tempest lay on us, all hope that we should be saved was then taken away.

ACTS 27:20

For this cause therefore have I called for you, to see you, and to speak with you: because that for the hope of Israel I am bound with this chain.

ACTS 28:20

And patience, experience; and experience, hope:

ROMANS 5:4

For we are saved by hope: but hope that is seen is not hope: for what a man seeth, why doth he yet hope for?

ROMANS 8:24

Or saith he it altogether for our sakes? For our sakes, no doubt, this is written: that he that ploweth should plow in hope; and that he that thresheth in hope should be partaker of his hope.

1 CORINTHIANS 9:10

And now abideth faith, hope, charity, these three; but the greatest of these is charity.

1 CORINTHIANS 13:13

If in this life only we have hope in Christ, we are of all men most miserable.

1 CORINTHIANS 15:19

And our hope of you is stedfast, knowing, that as ye are partakers of the sufferings, so shall ye be also of the consolation.

2 CORINTHIANS 1:7

Seeing then that we have such hope, we use great plainness of speech:

2 CORINTHIANS 3:12

For we through the Spirit wait for the hope of righteousness by faith.

GALATIANS 5:5

The eyes of your understanding being enlightened; that ye may know what is the hope of his calling, and what the riches of the glory of his inheritance in the saints.

EPHESIANS 1:18

That at that time ye were without Christ, being aliens from the commonwealth of Israel, and strangers from the covenants of promise, having no hope, and without God in the world:

EPHESIANS 2:12

For the hope which is laid up for you in heaven, whereof ye heard before in the word of the truth of the gospel;

COLOSSIANS 1:5

To whom God would make known what is the riches of the glory of this mystery among the Gentiles; which is Christ in you, the hope of glory:

COLOSSIANS 1:27

But I would not have you to be ignorant, brethren, concerning them which are asleep, that ye sorrow not, even as others which have no hope.

1 THESSALONIANS 1:3

But I would not have you to be ignorant, brethren, concerning them which are asleep, that ye sorrow not, even as others which have no hope.

1 THESSALONIANS 4:13

But let us, who are of the day, be sober, putting on the breastplate of faith and love; and for an helmet, the hope of salvation.

1 THESSALONIANS 5:8

Now our Lord Jesus Christ himself, and God, even our Father, which hath loved us, and hath given us everlasting consolation and good hope through grace.

2 THESSALONIANS 2:16

Titus 2:13 - Looking for that blessed hope, and the glorious appearing of the great God and our Saviour Jesus Christ;

TITUS 2:13

And we desire that every one of you do shew the same diligence to the full assurance of hope unto the end:

HEBREWS 6:11

That by two immutable things, in which it was impossible for God to lie, we might have a strong consolation, who have fled for refuge to lay hold upon the hope set before us: Which hope we have as an anchor of the soul, both sure and stedfast, and which entereth into that within the veil;

HEBREWS 6:18,19

Blessed be the God and Father of our Lord Jesus Christ, which according to his abundant mercy hath begotten us again unto a lively hope by the resurrection of Jesus Christ from the dead,

1 PETER 1:3

But sanctify the Lord God in your hearts: and be ready always to give an answer to every man that asketh you a reason of the hope that is in you with meekness and fear:

1 PETER 3:15

And every man that hath this hope in him purifieth himself, even as he is pure.

1 JOHN 3:3

LOVE

Thou shalt not avenge, nor bear any grudge against the children of thy people, but thou shalt love thy neighbour as thyself: I am the LORD.

LEVITICUS 19:18

And thou shalt love the LORD thy God with all thine heart, and with all thy soul, and with all thy might.

DEUTERONOMY 6:5

I am distressed for thee, my brother Jonathan: very pleasant hast thou been unto me: thy love to me was wonderful, passing the love of women.

2 SAMUEL 1:26

I will love thee, O LORD, my strength.

PSALM 18:1

LORD, I have loved the habitation of thy house, and the place where thine honour dwelleth.

PSALM 26:8

The seed also of his servants shall inherit it: and they that love his name shall dwell therein.

PSALM 69:36

Ye that love the LORD, hate evil: he preserveth the souls of his saints; he delivereth them out of the hand of the wicked.

PSALM 97:10

Pray for the peace of Jerusalem: they shall prosper that love thee.

PSALM 122:6

I love them that love me; and those that seek me early shall find me.

PROVERBS 8:17

Hatred stirreth up strifes: but love covereth all sins.

PROVERBS 10:12

Better is a dinner of herbs where love is, than a stalled ox and hatred therewith.

PROVERBS 15:17

He brought me to the banqueting house, and his banner over me was love.

SONG OF SOLOMON 2:4

I opened to my beloved; but my beloved had withdrawn himself, and was gone: my soul failed when he spake: I sought him, but I could not find him; I called him, but he gave me no answer.

SONG OF SOLOMON 5:6

Set me as a seal upon thine heart, as a seal upon thine arm: for love is strong as death; jealousy is cruel as the grave: the coals thereof are coals of fire, which hath a most vehement flame.

SONG OF SOLOMON 8:6

The LORD hath appeared of old unto me, saying, Yea, I have loved thee with an everlasting love: therefore with lovingkindness have I drawn thee.

JEREMIAH 31:3

But seek not Bethel, nor enter into Gilgal, and pass not to Beersheba: for Gilgal shall surely go into captivity, and Bethel shall come to nought.

AMOS 5:5

He hath shewed thee, O man, what is good; and what doth the LORD require of thee, but to do justly, and to love mercy, and to walk humbly with thy God?

MICAH 6:8

But I say unto you, Love your enemies, bless them that curse you, do good to them that hate you, and pray for them which despitefully use you, and persecute you;

MATTHEW 5:44

For if ye love them which love you, what reward have ye? do not even the publicans the same?

MATTHEW 5:46

And because iniquity shall abound, the love of many shall wax cold.

MATTHEW 24:12

But I know you, that ye have not the love of God in you.

JOHN 5:42

Therefore his sisters sent unto him, saying, Lord, behold, he whom thou lovest is sick.

JOHN 11:3

By this shall all men know that ye are my disciples, if ye have love one to another.

JOHN 13:35

This is my commandment, That ye love one another, as I have loved you. Greater love hath no man than this, that a man lay down his life for his friends.

JOHN 15:12,13

Who shall separate us from the love of Christ? shall tribulation, or distress, or persecution, or famine, or nakedness, or peril, or sword?

ROMANS 8:35

Owe no man any thing, but to love one another: for he that loveth another hath fulfilled the law.

ROMANS 13:8

For the love of Christ constraineth us; because we thus judge, that if one died for all, then were all dead:

2 CORINTHIANS 5:14

Finally, brethern, farewell. Be perfect, be of good comfort, be of one mind, live in peace; and the God of love and peace shall be with you.

2 CORINTHIANS 13:11

For in Jesus Christ neither circumcision availeth any thing, nor uncircumcision; but faith which worketh by love.

GALATIANS 5:6

But the fruit of the Spirit is love, joy, peace, longsuffering, gentleness, goodness, faith,

GALATIANS 5:22

But the fruit of the Spirit is love, joy, peace, longsuffering, gentleness, goodness, faith,

EPHESIANS 3:19

Grace be with all them that love our Lord Jesus Christ in sincerity. Amen.

EPHESIANS 6:24

If there be therefore any consolation in Christ, if any comfort of love, if any fellowship of the Spirit, if any bowels and mercies, Fulfil ye my joy, that ye be likeminded, having the same love, being of one accord, of one mind.

PHILIPPIANS 2:1,2

Remembering without ceasing your work of faith, and labour of love, and patience of hope in our Lord Jesus Christ, in the sight of God and our Father;

1 THESSALONIANS 1:3

For the love of money is the root of all evil: which while some coveted after, they have erred from the faith, and pierced themselves through with many sorrows.

1 TIMOTHY 6:10

For God hath not given us the spirit of fear; but of power, and of love, and of a sound mind.

2 TIMOTHY 1:7

And let us consider one another to provoke unto love and to good works:

HEBREWS 10:24

Let brotherly love continue.

HEBREWS 13:1

Whom having not seen, ye love; in whom, though now ye see him not, yet believing, ye rejoice with joy unspeakable and full of glory:

1 PETER 1:8

Seeing ye have purified your souls in obeying the truth through the Spirit unto unfeigned love of the brethren, see that ye love one another with a pure heart fervently:

1 PETER 1:22

Honour all men. Love the brotherhood. Fear God. Honour the king.

1 PETER 2:17

Behold, what manner of love the Father hath bestowed upon us, that we should be called the sons of God: therefore the world knoweth us not, because it knew him not.

1 JOHN 3:1

Beloved, let us love one another: for love is of God; and every one that loveth is born of God, and knoweth God.

1 JOHN 4:7

He that loveth not knoweth not God; for God is love.

1 JOHN 4:8

Nevertheless I have somewhat against thee, because thou hast left thy first love.

REVELATION 2:4

As many as I love, I rebuke and chasten: be zealous therefore, and repent.

REVELATION 3:19

HEAL...HEALED...HEALING

And Moses cried unto the Lord, saying, Heal her now, O God, I beseech thee.

NUMBERS 12:13

See now that I, even I, am he, and there is no god with me: I kill, and I make alive; I wound, and I heal: neither is there any that can deliver out of my hand.

DEUTERONOMY 32:39

So the waters were healed unto this day, according to the saying of Elisha which he spake.

2 KINGS 2:22

Then went he down, and dipped himself seven times in Jordan, according to the saying of the man of God: and his flesh came again like unto the flesh of a little child, and he was clean.

2 KINGS 5:14

And Hezekiah said unto Isaiah, What shall be the sign that the Lord will heal me, and that I shall go up into the house of the Lord the third day?

2 KINGS 20:8

And the Lord hearkened to Hezekiah, and healed the people.

2 CHRONICLES 30:20

Have mercy upon me, O Lord; for I am weak: O Lord, heal me; for my bones are vexed.

PSALM 6:2

O Lord my God, I cried unto thee, and thou hast healed me.

PSALM 30:2

I said, Lord, be merciful unto me: heal my soul; for I have sinned against thee.

PSALM 41:4

A time to kill, and a time to heal; a time to break down, and a time to build up;

ECCLESIASTES 3:3

But he was wounded for our transgressions, he was bruised for our iniquities: the chastisement of our peace was upon him; and with his stripes we are healed.

ISAIAH 53:5

Return, ye backsliding children, and I will heal your backslidings. Behold, we come unto thee; for thou art the LORD our God.

JEREMIAH 3:22

They have healed also the hurt of the daughter of my people slightly, saying, Peace, peace; when there is no peace.

JEREMAIH 6:14

Hast thou utterly rejected Judah? hath thy soul lothed Zion? why hast thou smitten us, and there is no healing for us? we looked for peace, and there is no good; and for the time of healing, and behold trouble!

JEREMIAH 14:19

Why is my pain perpetual, and my wound incurable, which refuseth to be healed? wilt thou be altogether unto me as a liar, and as waters that fail?

JEREMIAH 15:18

Heal me, O LORD, and I shall be healed; save me, and I shall be saved: for thou art my praise.

JEREMIAH 17:14

There is none to plead thy cause, that thou mayest be bound up: thou hast no healing medicines.

JEREMIAH 30:13

Then said he unto me, These waters issue out toward the east country, and go down into the desert, and go into the sea: which being brought forth into the sea, the waters shall be healed.

EZEKIEL 47:8

Come, and let us return unto the LORD: for he hath torn, and he will heal us; he hath smitten, and he will bind us up.

HOSEA 6:1

When I would have healed Israel, then the iniquity of Ephraim was discovered, and the wickedness of Samaria: for they commit falsehood; and the thief cometh in, and the troop of robbers spoileth without.

HOSEA 7:1

I will heal their backsliding, I will love them freely: for mine anger is turned away from him.

HOSEA 14:4

But unto you that fear my name shall the Sun of righteousness arise with healing in his wings; and ye shall go forth, and grow up as calves of the stall.

MALACHI 4:2

And Jesus went about all Galilee, teaching in their synagogues, and preaching the gospel of the kingdom, and healing all manner of sickness and all manner of disease among the people.

MATTHEW 4:23

And Jesus saith unto him, I will come and heal him.

MATTHEW 8:7

While he spake these things unto them, behold, there came a certain ruler, and worshipped him, saying, My daughter is even now dead: but come and lay thy hand upon her, and she shall live.

MATTHEW 9:18

And when he had called unto him his twelve disciples, he gave them power against unclean spirits, to cast them out, and to heal all manner of sickness and all manner of disease.

MATTHEW 10:1

And, behold, there was a man which had his hand withered. And they asked him, saying, Is it lawful to heal on the sabbath days? that they might accuse him.

MATTHEW 12:10

And, behold, a woman of Canaan came out of the same coasts, and cried unto him, saying, Have mercy on me, O Lord, thou son of David; my daughter is grievously vexed with a devil.

MATTHEW 15:22

And, behold, two blind men sitting by the way side, when they heard that Jesus passed by, cried out, saying, Have mercy on us, O Lord, thou son of David. And the multitude rebuked them, because they should hold their peace: but they cried the more, saying, Have mercy on us, O Lord, thou son of David. And Jesus stood still, and called them, and said, What will ye that I shall do unto you? They say unto him, Lord, that our eyes may be opened. So Jesus had compassion on them, and touched their eyes: and immediately their eyes received sight, and they followed him.

MATTHEW 20:30-34

And there came a leper to him, beseeching him, and kneeling down to him, and saying unto him, If thou wilt, thou canst make me clean.

MARK 1:40

And again he entered into Capernaum after some days; and it was noised that he was in the house.

MARK 2:1

And when he had looked round about on them with anger, being grieved for the hardness of their hearts, he saith unto the man, Stretch forth thine hand. And he stretched it out: and his hand was restored whole as the other.

MARK 3:5

And they began to pray him to depart out of their coasts.

MARK 5:17

And besought him greatly, saying, My little daughter lieth at the point of death: I pray thee, come and lay thy hands on her, that she may be healed; and she shall live.

MARK 5:23

And he cometh to Bethsaida; and they bring a blind man unto him, and besought him to touch him. And he took the blind man by the hand, and led him out of the town; and when he had spit on his eyes, and put his hands upon him, he asked him if he saw ought. And he looked up, and said, I see men as trees, walking. After that he put his hands again upon his eyes, and made him look up: and he was restored, and saw every man clearly.

MARK 8:22-25

The Spirit of the Lord is upon me, because he hath anointed me to preach the gospel to the poor; he hath sent me to heal the brokenhearted, to preach deliverance to the captives, and recovering of sight to the blind, to set at liberty them that are bruised,

LUKE 4:18

And it came to pass, when he was in a certain city, behold a man full of leprosy: who seeing Jesus fell on his face, and besought him, saying, Lord, if thou wilt, thou canst make me clean.

LUKE 5:12

And it came to pass on a certain day, as he was teaching, that there were Pharisees and doctors of the law sitting by, which were come out of every town of Galilee, and Judaea, and Jerusalem: and the power of the Lord was present to heal them.

LUKE 5:17

And the whole multitude sought to touch him: for there went virtue out of him, and healed them all.

LUKE 6:19

Now when he had ended all his sayings in the audience of the people, he entered into Capernaum.

LUKE 7:1

And when he heard of Jesus, he sent unto him the elders of the Jews, beseeching him that he would come and heal his servant.

LUKE 7:3

And they arrived at the country of the Gadarenes, which is over against Galilee.

LUKE 8:26

And a woman having an issue of blood twelve years, which had spent all her living upon physicians, neither could be healed of any,

LUKE 8:43

And when the woman saw that she was not hid, she came trembling, and falling down before him, she declared unto him before all the people for what cause she had touched him, and how she was healed immediately.

LUKE 8:47

And they departed, and went through the towns, preaching the gospel, and healing every where.

LUKE 9:6

And it came to pass, that on the next day, when they were come down from the hill, much people met him.

LUKE 9:37

And he was teaching in one of the synagogues on the sabbath. And, behold, there was a woman which had a spirit of infirmity eighteen years, and was bowed together, and could in no wise lift up herself. And when Jesus saw her, he called her to him, and said unto her, Woman, thou art loosed from thine infirmity. And he laid his hands on her: and immediately she was made straight, and glorified God.

LUKE 13:10-13

The Lord then answered him, and said, Thou hypocrite, doth not each one of you on the sabbath loose his ox or his ass from the stall, and lead him away to watering? And ought not this woman, being a daughter of Abraham, whom Satan hath bound, lo, these eighteen years, be loosed from this bond on the sabbath day?

LUKE 13:15,16

And as he entered into a certain village, there met him ten men that were lepers, which stood afar off: And they lifted up their voices, and said, Jesus, Master, have mercy on us. And when he saw them, he said unto them, Go shew yourselves unto the priests. And it came to pass, that, as they went, they were cleansed. And one of them, when he saw that he was healed, turned back, and with a loud voice glorified God, And fell down on his face at his feet, giving him thanks: and he was a Samaritan. And Jesus answering said, Were there not ten cleansed? but where are the nine? There are not found that returned to give glory to God, save this stranger.And he said unto him, Arise, go thy way: thy faith hath made thee whole.

LUKE 17:12-19

And it came to pass, that as he was come nigh unto Jericho, a certain blind man sat by the way side begging:

LUKE 18:35

And immediately he received his sight, and followed him, glorifying God: and all the people, when they saw it, gave praise unto God.

LUKE 18:43

And Jesus answered and said, Suffer ye thus far. And he touched his ear, and healed him.

LUKE 22:51

When he heard that Jesus was come out of Judaea into Galilee, he went unto him, and besought him that he would come down, and heal his son: for he was at the point of death.

JOHN 4:47

Now a certain man was sick, named Lazarus, of Bethany, the town of Mary and her sister Martha. (It was that Mary which anointed the Lord with ointment, and wiped his feet with her hair, whose brother Lazarus was sick.)

JOHN 11:1,2

And he that was dead came forth, bound hand and foot with graveclothes: and his face was bound about with a napkin. Jesus saith unto them, Loose him, and let him go.

JOHN 11:44

And beholding the man which was healed standing with them, they could say nothing against it.

ACTS 4:14

For the man was above forty years old, on whom this miracle of healing was shewed.

ACTS 4:22

By stretching forth thine hand to heal; and that signs and wonders may be done by the name of thy holy child Jesus.

ACTS 4:30

Insomuch that they brought forth the sick into the streets, and laid them on beds and couches, that at the least the shadow of Peter passing by might overshadow some of them. There came also a multitude out of the cities round about unto Jerusalem, bringing sick folks, and them which were vexed with unclean spirits: and they were healed every one.

ACTS 5:15,16

And there he found a certain man named Aeneas, which had kept his bed eight years, and was sick of the palsy. And Peter said unto him, Aeneas, Jesus Christ maketh thee whole: arise, and make thy bed. And he arose immediately. And all that dwelt at Lydda and Saron saw him, and turned to the Lord.

ACTS 9:33-35

How God anointed Jesus of Nazareth with the Holy Ghost and with power: who went about doing good, and healing all that were oppressed of the devil; for God was with him.

ACTS 10:38

The same heard Paul speak: who stedfastly beholding him, and perceiving that he had faith to be healed,

ACTS 14:9

And it came to pass, that the father of Publius lay sick of a fever and of a bloody flux: to whom Paul entered in, and prayed, and laid his hands on him, and healed him. So when this was done, others also, which had diseases in the island, came, and were healed:

ACTS 28:8,9

To another faith by the same Spirit; to another the gifts of healing by the same Spirit;

1 CORINTHIANS 12:9

And make straight paths for your feet, lest that which is lame be turned out of the way; but let it rather be healed.

HEBREWS 12:13

Confess your faults one to another, and pray one for another, that ye may be healed. The effectual fervent prayer of a righteous man availeth much.

JAMES 5:16

Who his own self bare our sins in his own body on the tree, that we, being dead to sins, should live unto righteousness: by whose stripes ye were healed.

1 PETER 2:24

And I saw one of his heads as it were wounded to death; and his deadly wound was healed: and all the world wondered after the beast.

REVELATION 13:3

In the midst of the street of it, and on either side of the river, was there the tree of life, which bare twelve manner of fruits, and yielded her fruit every month: and the leaves of the tree were for the healing of the nations.

REVELATION 22:2

SALVATION

And Moses said unto the people, Fear ye not, stand still, and see the salvation of the LORD, which he will shew to you to day: for the Egyptians whom ye have seen to day, ye shall see them again no more for ever.

EXODUS 14:13

Sing unto the LORD, all the earth; shew forth from day to day his salvation. Declare his glory among the heathen; his marvellous works among all nations.

1 CHRONICLES 16:23,24

Ye shall not need to fight in this battle: set yourselves, stand ye still, and see the salvation of the LORD with you, O Judah and Jerusalem: fear not, nor be dismayed; to morrow go out against them: for the LORD will be with you.

2 CHRONICLES 20:17

Salvation belongeth unto the LORD: thy blessing is upon thy people. Selah.

PSALM 3:8

Sing unto the LORD, bless his name; shew forth his salvation from day to day.

PSALM 96:2

The LORD is my strength and song, and is become my salvation.

PSALM 118:14

I will praise thee: for thou hast heard me, and art become my salvation.

PSALM 118:21

Salvation is far from the wicked: for they seek not thy statutes.

PSALM 119:155

Behold, God is my salvation; I will trust, and not be afraid: for the Lord Jehovah is my strength and my song; he also is become my salvation. Therefore with joy shall ye draw water out of the wells of salvation.

ISAIAH 12:2,3

In that day shall this song be sung in the land of Judah; We have a strong city; salvation will God appoint for walls and bulwarks.

ISAIAH 26:1

Rejoice greatly, O daughter of Zion; shout, O daughter of Jerusalem: behold, thy King cometh unto thee: he is just, and having salvation; lowly, and riding upon an ass, and upon a colt the foal of an ass.

ZECHARIAH 9:9

And hath raised up an horn of salvation for us in the house of his servant David; As he spake by the mouth of his holy prophets, which have been since the world began:

LUKE 1:69,70

Neither is there salvation in any other: for there is none other name under heaven given among men, whereby we must be saved.

ACTS 4:12

For I am not ashamed of the gospel of Christ: for it is the power of God unto salvation to every one that believeth; to the Jew first, and also to the Greek.

ROMANS 1:16

(For he saith, I have heard thee in a time accepted, and in the day of salvation have I succoured thee: behold, now is the accepted time; behold, now is the day of salvation.)

2 CORINTHIANS 6:2

Philippians 1:19 - For I know that this shall turn to my salvation through your prayer, and the supply of the Spirit of Jesus Christ,

PHILIPPIANS 1:19

And in nothing terrified by your adversaries: which is to them an evident token of perdition, but to you of salvation, and that of God.

PHILIPPIANS 1:28

How shall we escape, if we neglect so great salvation; which at the first began to be spoken by the Lord, and was confirmed unto us by them that heard him;

HEBREWS 2:3

So Christ was once offered to bear the sins of many; and unto them that look for him shall he appear the second time without sin unto salvation.

HEBREWS 9:28

Beloved, when I gave all diligence to write unto you of the common salvation, it was needful for me to write unto you, and exhort you that ye should earnestly contend for the faith which was once delivered unto the saints.

JUDE 1:3

And cried with a loud voice, saying, Salvation to our God which sitteth upon the throne, and unto the Lamb.

REVELATION 7:10

JOY

So David, and the elders of Israel, and the captains over thousands, went to bring up the ark of the covenant of the Lord out of the house of Obededom with joy.

1 CHRONICLES 15:25

So that the people could not discern the noise of the shout of joy from the noise of the weeping of the people: for the people shouted with a loud shout, and the noise was heard afar off.

EZRA 3:13

Then he said unto them, Go your way, eat the fat, and drink the sweet, and send portions unto them for whom nothing is prepared: for this day is holy unto our Lord: neither be ye sorry; for the joy of the Lord is your strength.

NEHEMIAH 8:10

The blessing of him that was ready to perish came upon me: and I caused the widow's heart to sing for joy.

JOB 29:13

Thou wilt shew me the path of life: in thy presence is fulness of joy; at thy right hand there are pleasures for evermore.

PSALM 16:11

For his anger endureth but a moment; in his favour is life: weeping may endure for a night, but joy cometh in the morning.

PSALM 30:5

When I remember these things, I pour out my soul in me: for I had gone with the multitude, I went with them to the house of God, with the voice of joy and praise, with a multitude that kept holyday.

PSALM 42:4

Then will I go unto the altar of God, unto God my exceeding joy: yea, upon the harp will I praise thee, O God my God.

PSALM 43:4

Beautiful for situation, the joy of the whole earth, is mount Zion, on the sides of the north, the city of the great King.

PSALM 48:2

O let the nations be glad and sing for joy: for thou shalt judge the people righteously, and govern the nations upon earth. Selah.

PSALM 67:4

They that sow in tears shall reap in joy.

PSALM 126:5

If I do not remember thee, let my tongue cleave to the roof of my mouth; if I prefer not Jerusalem above my chief joy.

PSALM 137:6

He that begetteth a fool doeth it to his sorrow: and the father of a fool hath no joy.

PROVERBS 17:21

Go thy way, eat thy bread with joy, and drink thy wine with a merry heart; for God now accepteth thy works.

ECCLESIASTES 9:7

Thou hast multiplied the nation, and not increased the joy: they joy before thee according to the joy in harvest, and as men rejoice when they divide the spoil.

ISAIAH 9:3

Therefore with joy shall ye draw water out of the wells of salvation.

ISAIAH 12:3

And the ransomed of the LORD shall return, and come to Zion with songs and everlasting joy upon their heads: they shall obtain joy and gladness, and sorrow and sighing shall flee away.

ISAIAH 35:10

Break forth into joy, sing together, ye waste places of Jerusalem: for the LORD hath comforted his people, he hath redeemed Jerusalem.

ISAIAH 52:9

Whereas thou has been forsaken and hated, so that no man went through thee, I will make thee an eternal excellency, a joy of many generations.

ISAIAH 60:15

To appoint unto them that mourn in Zion, to give unto them beauty for ashes, the oil of joy for mourning, the garment of praise for the spirit of heaviness; that they might be called trees of righteousness, the planting of the Lord, that he might be glorified.

ISAIAH 61:3

Behold, my servants shall sing for joy of heart, but ye shall cry for sorrow of heart, and shall howl for vexation of spirit.

ISAIAH 65:14

Thy words were found, and I did eat them; and thy word was unto me the joy and rejoicing of mine heart: for I am called by thy name, O Lord God of hosts.

JEREMIAH 15:16

Then shall the virgin rejoice in the dance, both young men and old together: for I will turn their mourning into joy, and will comfort them, and make them rejoice from their sorrow.

JEREMIAH 31:13

The voice of joy, and the voice of gladness, the voice of the bridegroom, and the voice of the bride, the voice of them that shall say, Praise the Lord of hosts: for the Lord is good; for his mercy endureth for ever: and of them that shall bring the sacrifice of praise into the house of the Lord. For I will cause to return the captivity of the land, as at the first, saith the Lord.

JEREMIAH 33:11

But he that received the seed into stony places, the same is he that heareth the word, and anon with joy receiveth it;

MATTHEW 13:20

Again, the kingdom of heaven is like unto treasure hid in a field; the which when a man hath found, he hideth, and for joy thereof goeth and selleth all that he hath, and buyeth that field.

MATTHEW 13:44

His lord said unto him, Well done, thou good and faithful servant: thou hast been faithful over a few things, I will make thee ruler over many things: enter thou into the joy of thy lord.

MATTHEW 25:21

For, lo, as soon as the voice of thy salutation sounded in mine ears, the babe leaped in my womb for joy.

LUKE 1:44

I say unto you, that likewise joy shall be in heaven over one sinner that repenteth, more than over ninety and nine just persons, which need no repentance.

LUKE 15:7

And while they yet believed not for joy, and wondered, he said unto them, Have ye here any meat?

LUKE 24:41

He that hath the bride is the bridegroom: but the friend of the bridegroom, which standeth and heareth him, rejoiceth greatly because of the bridegroom's voice: this my joy therefore is fulfilled.

JOHN 3:29

These things have I spoken unto you, that my joy might remain in you, and that your joy might be full.

JOHN 15:11

Verily, verily, I say unto you, That ye shall weep and lament, but the world shall rejoice: and ye shall be sorrowful, but your sorrow shall be turned into joy.

JOHN 16:20

And ye now therefore have sorrow: but I will see you again, and your heart shall rejoice, and your joy no man taketh from you.

JOHN 16:22

Hitherto have ye asked nothing in my name: ask, and ye shall receive, that your joy may be full.

JOHN 16:24

But none of these things move me, neither count I my life dear unto myself, so that I might finish my course with joy, and the ministry, which I have received of the Lord Jesus, to testify the gospel of the grace of God.

ACTS 20:24

For the kingdom of God is not meat and drink; but righteousness, and peace, and joy in the Holy Ghost.

ROMANS 14:17

Now the God of hope fill you with all joy and peace in believing, that ye may abound in hope, through the power of the Holy Ghost.

ROMANS 15:13

And I wrote this same unto you, lest, when I came, I should have sorrow from them of whom I ought to rejoice; having confidence in you all, that my joy is the joy of you all.

2 CORINTHIANS 2:3

But the fruit of the Spirit is love, joy, peace, longsuffering, gentleness, goodness, faith,

GALATIANS 5:22

Therefore, my brethren dearly beloved and longed for, my joy and crown, so stand fast in the Lord, my dearly beloved.

PHILIPPIANS 4:1

For ye are our glory and joy.

1 THESSALONIANS 2:20

Looking unto Jesus the author and finisher of our faith; who for the joy that was set before him endured the cross, despising the shame, and is set down at the right hand of the throne of God.

HEBREWS 12:2

My brethren, count it all joy when ye fall into divers temptations;

JAMES 1:2

Be afflicted, and mourn, and weep: let your laughter be turned to mourning, and your joy to heaviness.

JAMES 4:9

Whom having not seen, ye love; in whom, though now ye see him not, yet believing, ye rejoice with joy unspeakable and full of glory:

1 PETER 1:8

But rejoice, inasmuch as ye are partakers of Christ's sufferings; that, when his glory shall be revealed, ye may be glad also with exceeding joy.

1 PETER 4:13

PEACE

The LORD lift up his countenance upon thee, and give thee peace.
NUMBERS 6:26

When thou comest nigh unto a city to fight against it, then proclaim peace unto it.
DEUTERONOMY 20:10

And thus shall ye say to him that liveth in prosperity, Peace be both to thee, and peace be to thine house, and peace be unto all that thou hast.
1 SAMUEL 25:6

I will both lay me down in peace, and sleep: for thou, LORD, only makest me dwell in safety.
PSALM 4:8

The LORD will give strength unto his people; the LORD will bless his people with peace.
PSALM 29:11

Finally, brethren, farewell. Be perfect, be of good comfort, be of one mind, live in peace; and the God of love and peace shall be with you.
2 CORINTHIANS 13:11

For he is our peace, who hath made both one, and hath broken down the middle wall of partition between us;
EPHESIANS 2:14

Endeavouring to keep the unity of the Spirit in the bond of peace.
EPHESIANS 4:3

And the peace of God, which passeth all understanding, shall keep your hearts and minds through Christ Jesus.
PHILIPPIANS 4:7

To the saints and faithful brethren in Christ which are at Colosse: Grace be unto you, and peace, from God our Father and the Lord Jesus Christ.

COLOSSIANS 1:2

And let the peace of God rule in your hearts, to the which also ye are called in one body; and be ye thankful.

COLOSSIANS 3:15

And to esteem them very highly in love for their work's sake. And be at peace among yourselves.

1 THESSALONIANS 5:13

Now the Lord of peace himself give you peace always by all means. The Lord be with you all.

2 THESSALONIANS 3:16

And one of you say unto them, Depart in peace, be ye warmed and filled; notwithstanding ye give them not those things which are needful to the body; what doth it profit?

JAMES 2:16

Wherefore, beloved, seeing that ye look for such things, be diligent that ye may be found of him in peace, without spot, and blameless.

2 PETER 3:14

GRACE

Thou art fairer than the children of men: grace is poured into thy lips: therefore God hath blessed thee for ever.

PSALM 45:2

For they shall be an ornament of grace unto thy head, and chains about thy neck.

PROVERBS 1:9

So shall they be life unto thy soul, and grace to thy neck.

PROVERBS 3:22

Surely he scorneth the scorners: but he giveth grace unto the lowly.

PROVERBS 3:34

Who art thou, O great mountain? before Zerubbabel thou shalt become a plain: and he shall bring forth the headstone thereof with shoutings, crying, Grace, grace unto it.

ZECHARIAH 4:7

And the Word was made flesh, and dwelt among us, (and we beheld his glory, the glory as of the only begotten of the Father,) full of grace and truth.

JOIIN 1:14

And of his fulness have all we received, and grace for grace.

JOHN 1:16

For the law was given by Moses, but grace and truth came by Jesus Christ.

JOHN 1:17

And with great power gave the apostles witness of the resurrection of the Lord Jesus: and great grace was upon them all.

ACTS 4:33

Who, when he came, and had seen the grace of God, was glad, and exhorted them all, that with purpose of heart they would cleave unto the Lord.

ACTS 11:23

Long time therefore abode they speaking boldly in the Lord, which gave testimony unto the word of his grace, and granted signs and wonders to be done by their hands.

ACTS 14:3

To all that be in Rome, beloved of God, called to be saints: Grace to you and peace from God our Father, and the Lord Jesus Christ.

ROMANS 1:7

Being justified freely by his grace through the redemption that is in Christ Jesus:

ROMANS 3:24

Now to him that worketh is the reward not reckoned of grace, but of debt.

ROMANS 4:4

By whom also we have access by faith into this grace wherein we stand, and rejoice in hope of the glory of God.

ROMANS 5:2

Moreover the law entered, that the offence might abound. But where sin abounded, grace did much more abound:

ROMANS 5:20

What shall we say then? Shall we continue in sin, that grace may abound?

ROMANS 6:1

For sin shall not have dominion over you: for ye are not under the law, but under grace.

ROMANS 6:14

Even so then at this present time also there is a remnant according to the election of grace.

ROMANS 11:5

For if I by grace be a partaker, why am I evil spoken of for that for which I give thanks?

1 CORINTHIANS 10:30

Therefore, as ye abound in every thing, in faith, and utterance, and knowledge, and in all diligence, and in your love to us, see that ye abound in this grace also.

2 CORINTHIANS 8:7

For ye know the grace of our Lord Jesus Christ, that, though he was rich, yet for your sakes he became poor, that ye through his poverty might be rich.

2 CORINTHIANS 8:9

And God is able to make all grace abound toward you; that ye, always having all sufficiency in all things, may abound to every good work:

2 CORINTHIANS 9:8

And he said unto me, My grace is sufficient for thee: for my strength is made perfect in weakness. Most gladly therefore will I rather glory in my infirmities, that the power of Christ may rest upon me.

2 CORINTHIANS 12:9

I marvel that ye are so soon removed from him that called you into the grace of Christ unto another gospel:

GALATIANS 1:6

Christ is become of no effect unto you, whosoever of you are justified by the law; ye are fallen from grace.

GALATIANS 5:4

Even when we were dead in sins, hath quickened us together with Christ, (by grace ye are saved;)

EPHESIANS 2:5

Unto me, who am less than the least of all saints, is this grace given, that I should preach among the Gentiles the unsearchable riches of Christ;

EPHESIANS 3:8

Grace be with all them that love our Lord Jesus Christ in sincerity. Amen.

EPHESIANS 4:24

Let the word of Christ dwell in you richly in all wisdom; teaching and admonishing one another in psalms and hymns and spiritual songs, singing with grace In your hearts to the Lord.

COLOSSIANS 3:16

Let your speech be always with grace, seasoned with salt, that ye may know how ye ought to answer every man.

COLOSSIANS 4:6

Now our Lord Jesus Christ himself, and God, even our Father, which hath loved us, and hath given us everlasting consolation and good hope through grace,

2 THESSALONIANS 2:16

Unto Timothy, my own son in the faith: Grace, mercy, and peace, from God our Father and Jesus Christ our Lord.

1 TIMOTHY 1:2

Thou therefore, my son, be strong in the grace that is in Christ Jesus.

2 TIMOTHY 2:1

Let us therefore come boldly unto the throne of grace, that we may obtain mercy, and find grace to help in time of need.

HEBREWS 4:16

Wherefore we receiving a kingdom which cannot be moved, let us have grace, whereby we may serve God acceptably with reverence and godly fear: Of how much sorer punishment, suppose ye, shall he be thought worthy, who hath trodden under foot the Son of God, and hath counted the blood of the covenant, wherewith he was sanctified, an unholy thing, and hath done despite unto the Spirit of grace?

HEBREWS 10:28,29

But he giveth more grace. Wherefore he saith, God resisteth the proud, but giveth grace unto the humble.

JAMES 4:6

Likewise, ye husbands, dwell with them according to knowledge, giving honour unto the wife, as unto the weaker vessel, and as being heirs together of the grace of life; that your prayers be not hindered.

1 PETER 3:7

Likewise, ye younger, submit yourselves unto the elder. Yea, all of you be subject one to another, and be clothed with humility: for God resisteth the proud, and giveth grace to the humble.

1 PETER 5:5

But grow in grace, and in the knowledge of our Lord and Saviour Jesus Christ. To him be glory both now and for ever. Amen.

2 PETER 3:18

SANCTIFY / SANCTIFICATION

Sanctify unto me all the firstborn, whatsoever openeth the womb among the children of Israel, both of man and of beast: it is mine.

EXODUS 13:2

Keep the sabbath day to sanctify it, as the LORD thy God hath commanded thee.

DEUTERONOMY 5:12

And it was so, when the days of their feasting were gone about, that Job sent and sanctified them, and rose up early in the morning, and offered burnt offerings according to the number of them all: for Job said, It may be that my sons have sinned, and cursed God in their hearts. Thus did Job continually.

JOB 1:5

Before I formed thee in the belly I knew thee; and before thou camest forth out of the womb I sanctified thee, and I ordained thee a prophet unto the nations.

JEREMIAH 1:5

And I will sanctify my great name, which was profaned among the heathen, which ye have profaned in the midst of them; and the heathen shall know that I am the LORD, saith the Lord GOD, when I shall be sanctified in you before their eyes.

EZEKIEL 36:23

Sanctify ye a fast, call a solemn assembly, gather the elders and all the inhabitants of the land into the house of the LORD your God, and cry unto the LORD,

JOEL 1:14

Say ye of him, whom the Father hath sanctified, and sent into the world, Thou blasphemest; because I said, I am the Son of God?
JOHN 10:36

Sanctify them through thy truth: thy word is truth.
JOHN 17:17

And now, brethren, I commend you to God, and to the word of his grace, which is able to build you up, and to give you an inheritance among all them which are sanctified.
ACTS 20:32

That I should be the minister of Jesus Christ to the Gentiles, ministering the gospel of God, that the offering up of the Gentiles might be acceptable, being sanctified by the Holy Ghost.
ROMANS 15:16

But of him are ye in Christ Jesus, who of God is made unto us wisdom, and righteousness, and sanctification, and redemption:
1 CORINTHIANS 1:30

That he might sanctify and cleanse it with the washing of water by the word, That he might present it to himself a glorious church, not having spot, or wrinkle, or any such thing; but that it should be holy and without blemish.
EPHESIANS 5:26,27

And the very God of peace sanctify you wholly; and I pray God your whole spirit and soul and body be preserved blameless unto the coming of our Lord Jesus Christ.
1 THESSALONIANS 5:23

For it is sanctified by the word of God and prayer.
1 TIMOTHY 4:5

If a man therefore purge himself from these, he shall be a vessel unto honour, sanctified, and meet for the master's use, and prepared unto every good work.
2 TIMOTHY 2:21

By the which will we are sanctified through the offering of the body of Jesus Christ once for all.

Wherefore Jesus also, that he might sanctify the people with his own blood, suffered without the gate.

Elect according to the foreknowledge of God the Father, through sanctification of the Spirit, unto obedience and sprinkling of the blood of Jesus Christ: Grace unto you, and peace, be multiplied.

But sanctify the Lord God in your hearts: and be ready always to give an answer to every man that asketh you a reason of the hope that is in you with meekness and fear:

DELIVERANCE

And God sent me before you to preserve you a posterity in the earth, and to save your lives by a great deliverance.

GENESIS 45:7

Now Naaman, captain of the host of the king of Syria, was a great man with his master, and honourable, because by him the LORD had given deliverance unto Syria: he was also a mighty man in valour, but he was a leper.

2 KINGS 5:1

And he said, Open the window eastward. And he opened it. Then Elisha said, Shoot. And he shot. And he said, The arrow of the LORD's deliverance, and the arrow of deliverance from Syria: for thou shalt smite the Syrians in Aphek, till thou have consumed them.

2 KINGS 13:17

Thou art my hiding place; thou shalt preserve me from trouble; thou shalt compass me about with songs of deliverance. Selah.

PSALM 32:7

Thou art my King, O God: command deliverances for Jacob.

PSALM 44:4

The Spirit of the Lord is upon me, because he hath anointed me to preach the gospel to the poor; he hath sent me to heal the brokenhearted, to preach deliverance to the captives, and recovering of sight to the blind, to set at liberty them that are bruised, To preach the acceptable year of the Lord.

LUKE 4:18,19

Women received their dead raised to life again: and others were tortured, not accepting deliverance; that they might obtain a better resurrection:

HEBREWS 11:35

HOLY GHOST

Now the birth of Jesus Christ was on this wise: When as his mother Mary was espoused to Joseph, before they came together, she was found with child of the Holy Ghost.

MATTHEW 1:18

But while he thought on these things, behold, the angel of the LORD appeared unto him in a dream, saying, Joseph, thou son of David, fear not to take unto thee Mary thy wife: for that which is conceived in her is of the Holy Ghost.

MATTHEW 1:20

I indeed baptize you with water unto repentance. but he that cometh after me is mightier than I, whose shoes I am not worthy to bear: he shall baptize you with the Holy Ghost, and with fire:

MATTHEW 3:11

Wherefore I say unto you, All manner of sin and blasphemy shall be forgiven unto men: but the blasphemy against the Holy Ghost shall not be forgiven unto men.

MATTHEW 12:31

Go ye therefore, and teach all nations, baptizing them in the name of the Father, and of the Son, and of the Holy Ghost:

MATTHEW 28:19

I indeed have baptized you with water: but he shall baptize you with the Holy Ghost.

MARK 1:8

For David himself said by the Holy Ghost, The LORD said to my Lord, Sit thou on my right hand, till I make thine enemies thy footstool.

MARK 12:36

But when they shall lead you, and deliver you up, take no thought beforehand what ye shall speak, neither do ye premeditate: but whatsoever shall be given you in that hour, that speak ye: for it is not ye that speak, but the Holy Ghost.

MARK 13:11

For he shall be great in the sight of the Lord, and shall drink neither wine nor strong drink; and he shall be filled with the Holy Ghost, even from his mother's womb.

LUKE 1:15

And the angel answered and said unto her, The Holy Ghost shall come upon thee, and the power of the Highest shall overshadow thee: therefore also that holy thing which shall be born of thee shall be called the Son of God.

LUKE 1:35

And the Holy Ghost descended in a bodily shape like a dove upon him, and a voice came from heaven, which said, Thou art my beloved Son; in thee I am well pleased.

LUKE 3:22

And Jesus being full of the Holy Ghost returned from Jordan, and was led by the Spirit into the wilderness,

LUKE 4:1

For the Holy Ghost shall teach you in the same hour what ye ought to say.

LUKE 12:12

(But this spake he of the Spirit, which they that believe on him should receive: for the Holy Ghost was not yet given; because that Jesus was not yet glorified.)

JOHN 7:39

But the Comforter, which is the Holy Ghost, whom the Father will send in my name, he shall teach you all things, and bring all things to your remembrance, whatsoever I have said unto you.

JOHN 14:26

And now I am no more in the world, but these are in the world, and I come to thee. Holy Father, keep through thine own name those whom thou hast given me, that they may be one, as we are.

JOHN 17:11

And when he had said this, he breathed on them, and saith unto them, Receive ye the Holy Ghost:

JOHN 20:22

But ye shall receive power, after that the Holy Ghost is come upon you: and ye shall be witnesses unto me both in Jerusalem, and in all Judaea, and in Samaria, and unto the uttermost part of the earth.

ACTS 1:8

And they were all filled with the Holy Ghost, and began to speak with other tongues, as the Spirit gave them utterance.

ACTS 2:4

But Peter said, Ananias, why hath Satan filled thine heart to lie to the Holy Ghost, and to keep back part of the price of the land?

ACTS 5:3

Wherefore, brethren, look ye out among you seven men of honest report, full of the Holy Ghost and wisdom, whom we may appoint over this business.

ACTS 6:3

Ye stiffnecked and uncircumcised in heart and ears, ye do always resist the Holy Ghost: as your fathers did, so do ye.

ACTS 7:51

Who, when they were come down, prayed for them, that they might receive the Holy Ghost:

ACTS 8:15

Then had the churches rest throughout all Judaea and Galilee and Samaria, and were edified; and walking in the fear of the Lord, and in the comfort of the Holy Ghost, were multiplied.

ACTS 9:31

While Peter yet spake these words, the Holy Ghost fell on all them which heard the word. And they of the circumcision which believed were astonished, as many as came with Peter, because that on the Gentiles also was poured out the gift of the Holy Ghost.

ACTS 10:44,45

Can any man forbid water, that these should not be baptized, which have received the Holy Ghost as well as we?

ACTS 10:47

And as I began to speak, the Holy Ghost fell on them, as on us at the beginning. Then remembered I the word of the Lord, how that he said, John indeed baptized with water; but ye shall be baptized with the Holy Ghost.

ACTS 11:5,6

For he was a good man, and full of the Holy Ghost and of faith: and much people was added unto the Lord.

ACTS 11:24

And the disciples were filled with joy, and with the Holy Ghost.

ACTS 13:52

And God, which knoweth the hearts, bare them witness, giving them the Holy Ghost, even as he did unto us;

ACTS 15:8

He said unto them, Have ye received the Holy Ghost since ye believed? And they said unto him, We have not so much as heard whether there be any Holy Ghost.

ACTS 19:2

And when Paul had laid his hands upon them, the Holy Ghost came on them; and they spake with tongues, and prophesied.

ACTS 19:6

I say the truth in Christ, I lie not, my conscience also bearing me witness in the Holy Ghost,

ROMANS 9:1

For the kingdom of God is not meat and drink; but righteousness, and peace, and joy in the Holy Ghost.

ROMANS 14:17

Now the God of hope fill you with all joy and peace in believing, that ye may abound in hope, through the power of the Holy Ghost.

ROMANS 15:13

That I should be the minister of Jesus Christ to the Gentiles, ministering the gospel of God, that the offering up of the Gentiles might be acceptable, being sanctified by the Holy Ghost.

ROMANS 15:16

Which things also we speak, not in the words which man's wisdom teacheth, but which the Holy Ghost teacheth; comparing spiritual things with spiritual.

1 CORINTHIANS 2:13

For our gospel came not unto you in word only, but also in power, and in the Holy Ghost, and in much assurance; as ye know what manner of men we were among you for your sake. And ye became followers of us, and of the Lord, having received the word in much affliction, with joy of the Holy Ghost.

1 THESSALONIANS 1:5,6

Not by works of righteousness which we have done, but according to his mercy he saved us, by the washing of regeneration, and renewing of the Holy Ghost;

TITUS 3:5

For there are three that bear record in heaven, the Father, the Word, and the Holy Ghost: and these three are one.

1 JOHN 5:7

HOLY SPIRIT

And the earth was without form, and void; and darkness was upon the face of the deep. And the Spirit of God moved upon the face of the waters.

GENESIS 1:2

And the LORD said, My spirit shall not always strive with man, for that he also is flesh: yet his days shall be an hundred and twenty years.

GENESIS 6:3

The spirit of God hath made me, and the breath of the Almighty hath given me life.

JOB 33:4

Until the spirit be poured upon us from on high, and the wilderness be a fruitful field, and the fruitful field be counted for a forest.

ISAIAH 32:15

And Jesus, when he was baptized, went up straightway out of the water: and, lo, the heavens were opened unto him, and he saw the Spirit of God descending like a dove, and lighting upon him:

MATTHEW 3:16

Wherefore I say unto you, All manner of sin and blasphemy shall be forgiven unto men: but the blasphemy against the Holy Ghost shall not be forgiven unto men. And whosoever speaketh a word against the Son of man, it shall be forgiven him: but whosoever speaketh against the Holy Ghost, it shall not be forgiven him, neither in this world, neither in the world to come.

MATTHEW 12:31,32

Go ye therefore, and teach all nations, baptizing them in the name of the Father, and of the Son, and of the Holy Ghost:

MATTHEW 28:19

And Jesus being full of the Holy Ghost returned from Jordan, and was led by the Spirit into the wilderness,

LUKE 4:1

Jesus answered, Verily, verily, I say unto thee, Except a man be born of water and of the Spirit, he cannot enter into the kingdom of God. That which is born of the flesh is flesh; and that which is born of the Spirit is spirit.

JOHN 3:5,6

And I will pray the Father, and he shall give you another Comforter, that he may abide with you for ever; Even the Spirit of truth; whom the world cannot receive, because it seeth him not, neither knoweth him: but ye know him; for he dwelleth with you, and shall be in you.

JOHN 14:16,17

But the Comforter, which is the Holy Ghost, whom the Father will send in my name, he shall teach you all things, and bring all things to your remembrance, whatsoever I have said unto you.

JOHN 14:26

Howbeit when he, the Spirit of truth, is come, he will guide you into all truth: for he shall not speak of himself; but whatsoever he shall hear, that shall he speak: and he will shew you things to come.

JOHN 16:13

And it shall come to pass in the last days, saith God, I will pour out of my Spirit upon all flesh: and your sons and your daughters shall prophesy, and your young men shall see visions, and your old men shall dream dreams:

ACTS 2:17

But Peter said, Ananias, why hath Satan filled thine heart to lie to the Holy Ghost, and to keep back part of the price of the land? Whiles it remained, was it not thine own? and after it was sold, was it not in thine own power? why hast thou conceived this thing in thine heart? thou hast not lied unto men, but unto God.

ACTS 5:3,4

And declared to be the Son of God with power, according to the spirit of holiness, by the resurrection from the dead:

ROMANS 1:4

There is therefore now no condemnation to them which are in Christ Jesus, who walk not after the flesh, but after the Spirit. For the law of the Spirit of life in Christ Jesus hath made me free from the law of sin and death.

ROMANS 8:1,2

But ye are not in the flesh, but in the Spirit, if so be that the Spirit of God dwell in you. Now if any man have not the Spirit of Christ, he is none of his.

ROMANS 8:9

But if the Spirit of him that raised up Jesus from the dead dwell in you, he that raised up Christ from the dead shall also quicken your mortal bodies by his Spirit that dwelleth in you.

ROMANS 8:11

For ye have not received the spirit of bondage again to fear; but ye have received the Spirit of adoption, whereby we cry, Abba, Father. The Spirit itself beareth witness with our spirit, that we are the children of God:

ROMANS 8:15,16

Likewise the Spirit also helpeth our infirmities: for we know not what we should pray for as we ought: but the Spirit itself maketh intercession for us with groanings which cannot be uttered. And he that searcheth the hearts knoweth what is the mind of the Spirit, because he maketh intercession for the saints according to the will of God.

ROMANS 8:26,27

But the fruit of the Spirit is love, joy, peace, longsuffering, gentleness, goodness, faith, Meekness, temperance: against such there is no law.

GALATIANS 5:22,23

If we live in the Spirit, let us also walk in the Spirit. Let us not be desirous of vain glory, provoking one another, envying one another.

GALATIANS 5:25,26

And take the helmet of salvation, and the sword of the Spirit, which is the word of God:

EPHESIANS 6:17

But we are bound to give thanks alway to God for you, brethren beloved of the Lord, because God hath from the beginning chosen you to salvation through sanctification of the Spirit and belief of the truth:

2 THESSALONIANS 2:13

And without controversy great is the mystery of godliness: God was manifest in the flesh, justified in the Spirit, seen of angels, preached unto the Gentiles, believed on in the world, received up into glory.

1 TIMOTHY 3:16

How much more shall the blood of Christ, who through the eternal Spirit offered himself without spot to God, purge your conscience from dead works to serve the living God?

HEBREWS 9:14

If ye be reproached for the name of Christ, happy are ye; for the spirit of glory and of God resteth upon you: on their part he is evil spoken of, but on your part he is glorified.

1 PETER 4:14

SPIRITUAL GIFTS

For as the body is one, and hath many members, and all the members of that one body, being many, are one body: so also is Christ.For by one Spirit are we all baptized into one body, whether we be Jews or Gentiles, whether we be bond or free; and have been all made to drink into one Spirit. For the body is not one member, but many. If the foot shall say, Because I am not the hand, I am not of the body; is it therefore not of the body? And if the ear shall say, Because I am not the eye, I am not of the body; is it therefore not of the body? If the whole body were an eye, where were the hearing? If the whole were hearing, where were the smelling?

1 CORINTHIANS 12:12-17

But now hath God set the members every one of them in the body, as it hath pleased him. And if they were all one member, where were the body? But now are they many members, yet but one body. And the eye cannot say unto the hand, I have no need of thee: nor again the head to the feet, I have no need of you. Nay, much more those members of the body, which seem to be more feeble, are necessary: And those members of the body, which we think to be less honourable, upon these we bestow more abundant honour; and our uncomely parts have more abundant comeliness. For our comely parts have no need: but God hath tempered the body together, having given more abundant honour to that part which lacked.

1 CORINTHIANS 12:18-24

That there should be no schism in the body; but that the members should have the same care one for another. And whether one member suffer, all the members suffer with it; or one member be honoured, all the members rejoice with it. Now ye are the body of Christ, and members in particular. And God hath set some in the church, first apostles, secondarily prophets, thirdly teachers, after that miracles, then gifts of healings, helps, governments, diversities of tongues. Are all apostles? are all prophets? are all teachers? are all workers of miracles? Have all the gifts of healing? do all speak with tongues? do all interpret? But covet earnestly the best gifts: and yet shew I unto you a more excellent way.

1 CORINTHIANS 12:25-31

TONGUES

And Moses said unto the Lord, O my Lord, I am not eloquent, neither
heretofore, nor since thou hast unto thy servant: but I am slow of speech,
and of a slow tongue.

EXODUS 4:10

And my tongue shall speak of thy righteousness and of thy praise all the
day long.

PSALM 35:28

The mouth of the righteous speaketh wisdom, and his tongue talketh
of judgment.

PSALM 37:30

I said, I will take heed to my ways, that I sin not with my tongue: I will keep
my mouth with a bridle, while the wicked is before me.

PSALM 39:1

My tongue shall speak of thy word: for all thy commandments
are righteousness.

PSALM 119:72

Then was our mouth filled with laughter, and our tongue with singing: then
said they among the heathen, The Lord hath done great things for them.

PSALM 126:2

For there is not a word in my tongue, but, lo, O Lord, thou knowest
it altogether.

PSALM 139:4

They have sharpened their tongues like a serpent; adders' poison is under
their lips. Selah.

PSALM 140:3

The tongue of the wise useth knowledge aright: but the mouth of fools poureth out foolishness.

PROVERBS 15:2

A wholesome tongue is a tree of life: but perverseness therein is a breach in the spirit.

PROVERBS 15:4

He that hath a froward heart findeth no good: and he that hath a perverse tongue falleth into mischief.

PROVERBS 17:20

She openeth her mouth with wisdom; and in her tongue is the law of kindness.

PROVERBS 31:26

Thou shalt not see a fierce people, a people of a deeper speech than thou canst perceive; of a stammering tongue, that thou canst not understand.

ISAIAH 33:19

Follow after charity, and desire spiritual gifts, but rather that ye may prophesy. For he that speaketh in an unknown tongue speaketh not unto men, but unto God: for no man understandeth him; howbeit in the spirit he speaketh mysteries. But he that prophesieth speaketh unto men to edification, and exhortation, and comfort. He that speaketh in an unknown tongue edifieth himself; but he that prophesieth edifieth the church. I would that ye all spake with tongues but rather that ye prophesied: for greater is he that prophesieth than he that speaketh with tongues, except he interpret, that the church may receive edifying.

1 CORINTHIANS 14:1-5

Even so the tongue is a little member, and boasteth great things. Behold, how great a matter a little fire kindleth! And the tongue is a fire, a world of iniquity: so is the tongue among our members, that it defileth the whole body, and setteth on fire the course of nature; and it is set on fire of hell.

JAMES 3:5,6

HOLY CALLING

For the gifts and calling of God are without repentance.

ROMANS 11:29

Let every man abide in the same calling wherein he was called.

1 CORINTHIANS 7:20

The eyes of your understanding being enlightened; that ye may know what is the hope of his calling, and what the riches of the glory of his inheritance in the saints,

EPHESIANS 1:18

I press toward the mark for the prize of the high calling of God in Christ Jesus.

PHILIPPIANS 3:14

Who hath saved us, and called us with an holy calling, not according to our works, but according to his own purpose and grace, which was given us in Christ Jesus before the world began, But is now made manifest by the appearing of our Saviour Jesus Christ, who hath abolished death, and hath brought life and immortality to light through the gospel: Whereunto I am appointed a preacher, and an apostle, and a teacher of the Gentiles.

2 TIMOTHY 1:9-11

Wherefore, holy brethren, partakers of the heavenly calling, consider the Apostle and High Priest of our profession, Christ Jesus;

HEBREWS 3:11

Wherefore the rather, brethren, give diligence to make your calling and election sure: for if ye do these things, ye shall never fall:

2 PETER 1:10

ABUNDANT SUPPLY

And the Lord passed by before him, and proclaimed, The Lord, The Lord God, merciful and gracious, longsuffering, and abundant in goodness and truth, Keeping mercy for thousands, forgiving iniquity and transgression and sin, and that will by no means clear the guilty; visiting the iniquity of the fathers upon the children, and upon the children's children, unto the third and to the fourth generation.

EXODUS 34:6,7

And she gave the king an hundred and twenty talents of gold, and of spices very great store, and precious stones: there came no more such abundance of spices as these which the queen of Sheba gave to king Solomon.

1 KINGS 10:10

And Elijah said unto Ahab, Get thee up, eat and drink; for there is a sound of abundance of rain.

1 KINGS 18:41

And David prepared iron in abundance for the nails for the doors of the gates, and for the joinings; and brass in abundance without weight; Also cedar trees in abundance: for the Zidonians and they of Tyre brought much cedar wood to David.

1 CHRONICLES 22:3,4

And after certain years he went down to Ahab to Samaria. And Ahab killed sheep and oxen for him in abundance, and for the people that he had with him, and persuaded him to go up with him to Ramothgilead.

2 CHRONICLES 18:2

Now it came to pass, that at what time the chest was brought unto the king's office by the hand of the Levites, and when they saw that there was much money, the king's scribe and the high priest's officer came and emptied the chest, and took it, and carried it to his place again. Thus they did day by day, and gathered money in abundance.

2 CHRONICLES 24:11

Also he strengthened himself, and built up all the wall that was broken, and raised it up to the towers, and another wall without, and repaired Millo in the city of David, and made darts and shields in abundance.

2 CHRONICLES 32:5

Moreover he provided him cities, and possessions of flocks and herds in abundance: for God had given him substance very much.

2 CHRONICLES 32:39

And they took strong cities, and a fat land, and possessed houses full of all goods, wells digged, vineyards, and oliveyards, and fruit trees in abundance: so they did eat, and were filled, and became fat, and delighted themselves in thy great goodness.

NEHEMIAH 9:25

But the meek shall inherit the earth; and shall delight themselves in the abundance of peace.

PSALM 37:11

Lo, this is the man that made not God his strength; but trusted in the abundance of his riches, and strengthened himself in his wickedness.

PSALM 52:7

In his days shall the righteous flourish; and abundance of peace so long as the moon endureth.

PSALM 72:7

Let the wicked forsake his way, and the unrighteous man his thoughts: and let him return unto the LORD, and he will have mercy upon him; and to our God, for he will abundantly pardon.

ISAIAH 55:7

Come ye, say they, I will fetch wine, and we will fill ourselves with strong drink; and to morrow shall be as this day, and much more abundant.

ISAIAH 56:12

By reason of the abundance of his horses their dust shall cover thee: thy walls shall shake at the noise of the horsemen, and of the wheels, and of the chariots, when he shall enter into thy gates, as men enter into a city wherein is made a breach.

EZEKIEL 26:10

For if by one man's offence death reigned by one; much more they which receive abundance of grace and of the gift of righteousness shall reign in life by one, Jesus Christ.)

ROMANS 5:17

Are they ministers of Christ? (I speak as a fool) I am more; in labours more abundant, in stripes above measure, in prisons more frequent, in deaths oft.

2 CORINTHIANS 11:23

Now unto him that is able to do exceeding abundantly above all that we ask or think, according to the power that worketh in us,

EPHESIANS 3:20

And the grace of our Lord was exceeding abundant with faith and love which is in Christ Jesus.

1 TIMOTHY 1:14

Blessed be the God and Father of our Lord Jesus Christ, which according to his abundant mercy hath begotten us again unto a lively hope by the resurrection of Jesus Christ from the dead,

1 PETER 1:3

ABOVE:
Hubert & Ruth Cash
1971

RIGHT:
Ruth Cash
2015

FRONT COVER:
Hubert & Ruth Cash
1981

56379519R00088

Made in the USA
Charleston, SC
20 May 2016